# FOURIER TRANSFORMS

**Sudhanshu Aggarwal**
*M.Sc., CSIR-NET, Ph.D.*
Assistant Professor & Head
Department of Mathematics
National Post Graduate College, Barhalganj
Gorakhpur, Uttar Pradesh, India

# PREFACE

Fourier transform is one of the most important and often used integral transform. It is frequently applied for attaining the solutions to the problems of science and engineering such as image analysis, image filtering, image reconstruction, image compression, signal analyzing and circuit analysis. This transform is also effectively applied to initial and boundary value problems.

This book is to explore the basic concepts of Fourier transforms in a simple, systematic and easy-to-understand manner. The present book is divided into six chapters which cover all the important topics like Fourier transform, Fourier sine transform, Fourier cosine transform, finite Fourier sine transform, finite Fourier cosine transform and application of Fourier transforms.

**Chapter 1** presents the introduction of Fourier transform. The definition of Fourier transform, inverse Fourier transform, properties of Fourier transform (Linearity; Damping; Shifting; Modulation; Derivative and Convolution) are presented in a brief manner in this chapter.

**Chapter 2** deals with Fourier sine transform and inverse Fourier sine transform.

**Chapter 3** discusses the Fourier cosine transform and inverse Fourier cosine transform.

**Chapter 4** discusses the finite Fourier sine transform and inverse finite Fourier sine transform.

**Chapter 5** discusses the finite Fourier cosine transform and inverse finite Fourier cosine transform.

**Chapter 6** deals with the applications of Fourier transforms for solving partial differential equations.

I hope that this book is very useful for students. I heartily welcome valuable comments and suggestions from my readers for the improvement of this book, which may be addressed to sudhanshu30187@gmail.com.

**Dr. Sudhanshu Aggarwal**

# CONTENTS

**PREFACE**

| CHAPTER | TITLE | PAGE NO. |
|---|---|---|
| 1. | Fourier Transform | 5-28 |
| 2. | Fourier Sine Transform | 29-38 |
| 3. | Fourier Cosine Transform | 39-46 |
| 4. | Finite Fourier Sine Transform | 47-56 |
| 5. | Finite Fourier Cosine Transform | 57-64 |
| 6. | Applications of Fourier Transforms | 65-96 |
|  | Appendix | 97-98 |
|  | References | 99 |

# Chapter-1

# FOURIER TRANSFORM

**Introduction:** Integral transforms are useful in solving initial and boundary vale problems and in evaluating certain integrals. In this chapter, we shall define Fourier transform, inverse Fourier transform and their properties. In the last section of this chapter, we have solved numerical problems related them.

**Fourier Transform:** The Fourier transform of $F(x)$, denoted by $F\{F(x)\}$, is defined by

$$F\{F(x)\} = \int_{-\infty}^{\infty} F(x) e^{ipx} \, dx = f(p)$$

**Inverse Fourier Transform:** The inverse Fourier transform of $f(p)$, denoted by $F^{-1}\{f(p)\}$, is defined by

$$F^{-1}\{f(p)\} = \frac{1}{2\pi} \int_{-\infty}^{\infty} f(p) e^{-ipx} \, dp = F(x)$$

**Existence of Fourier Transform:** The following conditions are sufficient for the existence of the Fourier transform of a function $F(x)$:

1. $F(x)$ is piecewise continuous on every finite interval.
2. $F(x)$ is absolutely integrable for all $x$.

# Alternative Definitions of Fourier Transform

**Definition: 1**

**Fourier Transform:** The Fourier transform of $F(x)$, denoted by $F\{F(x)\}$, is defined by

$$F\{F(x)\} = \frac{1}{2\pi} \int_{-\infty}^{\infty} F(x) e^{ipx} \, dx = f(p)$$

**Inverse Fourier Transform:** The inverse Fourier transform of $f(p)$, denoted by $F^{-1}\{f(p)\}$, is defined by

$$F^{-1}\{f(p)\} = \int_{-\infty}^{\infty} f(p) e^{-ipx} \, dp = F(x)$$

**Definition: 2**

**Fourier Transform:** The Fourier transform of $F(x)$, denoted by $F\{F(x)\}$, is defined by

$$F\{F(x)\} = \frac{1}{\sqrt{2\pi}} \int_{-\infty}^{\infty} F(x) e^{ipx} \, dx = f(p)$$

**Inverse Fourier Transform:** The inverse Fourier transform of $f(p)$, denoted by $F^{-1}\{f(p)\}$, is defined by

$$F^{-1}\{f(p)\} = \frac{1}{\sqrt{2\pi}} \int_{-\infty}^{\infty} f(p)e^{-ipx}\, dp = F(x)$$

**Properties of Fourier Transform**

1. **Linearity Property:** If $F\{F(x)\} = f(p)$ and $F\{G(x)\} = g(p)$ then

$$F\{aF(x) + bG(x)\} = aF\{F(x)\} + bF\{G(x)\} = af(p) + bg(p)$$

where $a$ and $b$ are any constants.

**Proof:** By the definition of Fourier transform, we have

$$F\{F(x)\} = \int_{-\infty}^{\infty} F(x)e^{ipx}\, dx$$

$$\Rightarrow F\{aF(x) + bG(x)\} = \int_{-\infty}^{\infty} [aF(x) + bG(x)]e^{ipx}\, dx$$

$$\Rightarrow F\{aF(x) + bG(x)\} = \int_{-\infty}^{\infty} [aF(x)]e^{ipx}\, dx + \int_{-\infty}^{\infty} [bG(x)]e^{ipx}\, dx$$

$$\Rightarrow F\{aF(x) + bG(x)\} = a\int_{-\infty}^{\infty} F(x)e^{ipx}\, dx + b\int_{-\infty}^{\infty} G(x)e^{ipx}\, dx$$

$$\Rightarrow F\{aF(x) + bG(x)\} = aF\{F(x)\} + bF\{G(x)\} = af(p) + bg(p)$$

2. **Change of Scale Property or Damping Property:** If $F\{F(x)\} = f(p)$ then

$$F\{F(ax)\} = \frac{1}{a} f\left(\frac{p}{a}\right), a \neq 0$$

**Proof:** By the definition of Fourier transform, we have

$$F\{F(x)\} = \int_{-\infty}^{\infty} F(x)e^{ipx}\, dx = f(p)$$

$$\Rightarrow F\{F(ax)\} = \int_{-\infty}^{\infty} F(ax)e^{ipx}\, dx$$

Put $ax = t \Rightarrow dx = \frac{dt}{a}$ in R.H.S. of above equation, we have

$$F\{F(ax)\} = \int_{-\infty}^{\infty} F(t)e^{i\left(\frac{p}{a}\right)t} \frac{dt}{a} = \frac{1}{a} f\left(\frac{p}{a}\right), a \neq 0$$

3. **Shifting Property:** If $F\{F(x)\} = f(p)$ then $F\{F(x-a)\} = e^{iap} f(p)$

   **Proof:** By the definition of Fourier transform, we have

   $$F\{F(x)\} = \int_{-\infty}^{\infty} F(x)e^{ipx}\, dx = f(p)$$

   $$\Rightarrow F\{F(x-a)\} = \int_{-\infty}^{\infty} F(x-a)e^{ipx}\, dx$$

   Put $x - a = t \Rightarrow dx = dt$ in R.H.S. of above equation, we have

   $$F\{F(x-a)\} = \int_{-\infty}^{\infty} F(t)e^{ip(t+a)}\, dt$$

   $$\Rightarrow F\{F(x-a)\} = e^{iap} \int_{-\infty}^{\infty} F(t)e^{ipt}\, dt = e^{iap} f(p)$$

4. **Modulation Theorem:** If $F\{F(x)\} = f(p)$ then

   $$F\{F(x)\cos ax\} = \frac{1}{2}[f(p+a) + f(p-a)]$$

**Proof:** By the definition of Fourier transform, we have

$$F\{F(x)\} = \int_{-\infty}^{\infty} F(x)e^{ipx}\,dx = f(p)$$

$$\Rightarrow F\{F(x)\cos ax\} = \int_{-\infty}^{\infty} e^{ipx} F(x)\cos ax\,dx$$

$$\Rightarrow F\{F(x)\cos ax\} = \int_{-\infty}^{\infty} e^{ipx} F(x)\left[\frac{e^{iax}+e^{-iax}}{2}\right]dx$$

$$\Rightarrow F\{F(x)\cos ax\} = \frac{1}{2}\left[\int_{-\infty}^{\infty} e^{ipx} F(x)e^{iax}\,dx + \int_{-\infty}^{\infty} e^{ipx} F(x)e^{-iax}\,dx\right]$$

$$\Rightarrow F\{F(x)\cos ax\} = \frac{1}{2}\left[\int_{-\infty}^{\infty} e^{i(p+a)x} F(x)\,dx + \int_{-\infty}^{\infty} e^{i(p-a)x} F(x)\,dx\right]$$

$$\Rightarrow F\{F(x)\cos ax\} = \frac{1}{2}[f(p+a) + f(p-a)]$$

**Fourier Transforms of Derivatives:** If $F\{F(x)\} = f(p)$ then

$$F\{F^{(n)}(x)\} = (-1)^n (ip)^n f(p)$$

where $F(x)$ and all its derivatives vanish at infinity.

**Proof:** By the definition of Fourier transform, we have

$$F\{F(x)\} = \int_{-\infty}^{\infty} F(x)e^{ipx}\,dx = f(p)$$

$$\Rightarrow F\{F'(x)\} = \int_{-\infty}^{\infty} F'(x)e^{ipx}\,dx$$

$$\Rightarrow F\{F'(x)\} = \left[F(x)e^{ipx}\right]_{-\infty}^{\infty} - \int_{-\infty}^{\infty}(ip)F(x)e^{ipx}\,dx$$

$$\Rightarrow F\{F'(x)\} = 0 - (ip)\int_{-\infty}^{\infty} F(x)e^{ipx}\,dx$$

$$\Rightarrow F\{F'(x)\} = -(ip)\int_{-\infty}^{\infty} F(x)e^{ipx}\,dx$$

$$\Rightarrow F\{F'(x)\} = -(ip)f(p)$$

Now, $F\{F''(x)\} = \int_{-\infty}^{\infty} F''(x)e^{ipx}\,dx$

$$\Rightarrow F\{F''(x)\} = \left[F'(x)e^{ipx}\right]_{-\infty}^{\infty} - \int_{-\infty}^{\infty}(ip)F'(x)e^{ipx}\,dx$$

$$\Rightarrow F\{F''(x)\} = 0 - \int_{-\infty}^{\infty}(ip)F'(x)e^{ipx}\,dx$$

$$\Rightarrow F\{F''(x)\} = -(ip)\int_{-\infty}^{\infty}(ip)F'(x)e^{ipx}\,dx$$

$$\Rightarrow F\{F''(x)\} = -(ip)F\{F'(x)\}$$

$$\Rightarrow F\{F''(x)\} = -(ip)[-(ip)f(p)]$$

$$\Rightarrow F\{F''(x)\} = (-1)^2(ip)^2 f(p)$$

Proceeding in the same way, we have

$$F\{F^{(n)}(x)\} = (-1)^n (ip)^n f(p)$$

**Convolution of Two Functions:** The convolution of two functions $F(x)$ and $G(x)$ over the interval $(-\infty, \infty)$ is denoted by $F * G$ and it is defined by

$$F * G = \int_{-\infty}^{\infty} F(x-u)G(u)\, du$$

**Convolution Theorem:** If $F\{F(x)\} = f(p)$ and $F\{G(x)\} = g(p)$ then

$$F\{F(x) * G(x)\} = F\{F(x)\}F\{G(x)\} = f(p)g(p)$$

**Proof:** By the definition of Fourier transform, we have

$$F\{F(x)\} = \int_{-\infty}^{\infty} F(x)e^{ipx}\, dx = f(p)$$

$$\Rightarrow F\{F(x) * G(x)\} = \int_{-\infty}^{\infty} e^{ipx} [F(x) * G(x)]\, dx$$

$$\Rightarrow F\{F(x) * G(x)\} = \int_{-\infty}^{\infty} e^{ipx} \left[ \int_{-\infty}^{\infty} F(x-u)G(u)du \right] dx$$

By changing the order of integration, we have

$$F\{F(x) * G(x)\} = \int_{-\infty}^{\infty} G(u) \left[ \int_{-\infty}^{\infty} F(x-u)e^{ipx}\, dx \right] du$$

Put $x - u = t \Rightarrow dx = dt$, we have

$$F\{F(x) * G(x)\} = \int_{-\infty}^{\infty} G(u) \left[ \int_{-\infty}^{\infty} F(t) e^{ip(t+u)} dt \right] du$$

$$\Rightarrow F\{F(x) * G(x)\} = \int_{-\infty}^{\infty} G(u) e^{ipu} \left[ \int_{-\infty}^{\infty} F(t) e^{ipt} dt \right] du$$

$$\Rightarrow F\{F(x) * G(x)\} = \int_{-\infty}^{\infty} G(u) e^{ipu} [F\{F(x)\}] du$$

$$\Rightarrow F\{F(x) * G(x)\} = F\{F(x)\} F\{G(x)\} = f(p) g(p)$$

**Example: 1** Find the Fourier transform of

$$F(x) = \begin{cases} 1, & |x| < 1 \\ 0, & |x| > 1 \end{cases}$$

Hence evaluate $\int_0^\infty \frac{\sin x}{x} dx$.

**Solution:** By the definition of Fourier transform, we have

$$F\{F(x)\} = \int_{-\infty}^{\infty} F(x) e^{ipx} dx$$

$$\Rightarrow F\{F(x)\} = \int_{-\infty}^{-1} F(x) e^{ipx} dx + \int_{-1}^{1} F(x) e^{ipx} dx + \int_{1}^{\infty} F(x) e^{ipx} dx$$

By the given definition of $F(x)$, we have

$$F\{F(x)\} = \int_{-\infty}^{-1} 0 \cdot e^{ipx} dx + \int_{-1}^{1} 1 \cdot e^{ipx} dx + \int_{1}^{\infty} 0 \cdot e^{ipx} dx$$

$$\Rightarrow F\{F(x)\} = \int_{-1}^{1} e^{ipx}\, dx = \left[\frac{e^{ipx}}{ip}\right]_{-1}^{1} = \left[\frac{e^{ip}}{ip} - \frac{e^{-ip}}{ip}\right] = \frac{2}{p}\sin p, p \neq 0$$

By the inverse Fourier transform, we have

$$F^{-1}\{f(p)\} = \frac{1}{2\pi}\int_{-\infty}^{\infty} f(p)e^{-ipx}\, dp = F(x)$$

$$\Rightarrow F(x) = \frac{1}{2\pi}\int_{-\infty}^{\infty} e^{-ipx}\left(\frac{2}{p}\sin p\right) dp$$

$$\Rightarrow \begin{cases} 1, & |x| < 1 \\ 0, & |x| > 1 \end{cases} = \frac{1}{\pi}\int_{-\infty}^{\infty} e^{-ipx}\left(\frac{\sin p}{p}\right) dp$$

Putting $x = 0$, we get

$$\frac{1}{\pi}\int_{-\infty}^{\infty} \left(\frac{\sin p}{p}\right) dp = 1$$

$$\Rightarrow \int_{-\infty}^{\infty} \left(\frac{\sin p}{p}\right) dp = \pi$$

Since the integrand namely $\left(\frac{\sin p}{p}\right)$ is an even function in the interval $(-\infty, \infty)$, so we have

$$\int_{0}^{\infty} \frac{\sin x}{x}\, dx = \frac{\pi}{2}$$

**Example: 2** Show that the Fourier transform of $e^{-\left(\frac{x^2}{2}\right)}$ is reciprocal.

**Solution:** By the definition of Fourier transform, we have

$$F\{F(x)\} = \frac{1}{\sqrt{2\pi}} \int_{-\infty}^{\infty} F(x) e^{ipx} \, dx$$

$$\Rightarrow F\left\{e^{-\left(\frac{x^2}{2}\right)}\right\} = \frac{1}{\sqrt{2\pi}} \int_{-\infty}^{\infty} e^{-\left(\frac{x^2}{2}\right)} e^{ipx} \, dx$$

$$\Rightarrow F\left\{e^{-\left(\frac{x^2}{2}\right)}\right\} = \frac{1}{\sqrt{2\pi}} \int_{-\infty}^{\infty} e^{-\left(\frac{1}{2}\right)(x^2 - 2ipx)} \, dx$$

$$\Rightarrow F\left\{e^{-\left(\frac{x^2}{2}\right)}\right\} = \frac{1}{\sqrt{2\pi}} \int_{-\infty}^{\infty} e^{-\left(\frac{1}{2}\right)[x^2 - 2ipx + (ip)^2 - (ip)^2]} \, dx$$

$$\Rightarrow F\left\{e^{-\left(\frac{x^2}{2}\right)}\right\} = \frac{1}{\sqrt{2\pi}} e^{-\left(\frac{p^2}{2}\right)} \int_{-\infty}^{\infty} e^{-\left(\frac{1}{2}\right)[x - ip]^2} \, dx$$

Put $[x - ip] = t \Rightarrow dx = dt$ in the R.H.S. of above equation, we have

$$F\left\{e^{-\left(\frac{x^2}{2}\right)}\right\} = \frac{1}{\sqrt{2\pi}} e^{-\left(\frac{p^2}{2}\right)} \int_{-\infty}^{\infty} e^{-\left(\frac{t^2}{2}\right)} \, dt$$

Since the integrand namely $e^{-\left(\frac{t^2}{2}\right)}$ is an even function in the interval $(-\infty, \infty)$, so we have

$$F\left\{e^{-\left(\frac{x^2}{2}\right)}\right\} = \frac{2}{\sqrt{2\pi}} e^{-\left(\frac{p^2}{2}\right)} \int_{0}^{\infty} e^{-\left(\frac{t^2}{2}\right)} \, dt$$

Put $\frac{t^2}{2} = u \Rightarrow tdt = du \Rightarrow dt = \frac{du}{\sqrt{2u}}$ in the R.H.S. of above equation, we have

$$F\left\{e^{-\left(\frac{x^2}{2}\right)}\right\} = \frac{2}{\sqrt{2\pi}} e^{-\left(\frac{p^2}{2}\right)} \int_0^\infty e^{-u} \frac{du}{\sqrt{2u}}$$

$$\Rightarrow F\left\{e^{-\left(\frac{x^2}{2}\right)}\right\} = \frac{1}{\sqrt{\pi}} e^{-\left(\frac{p^2}{2}\right)} \int_0^\infty e^{-u} u^{\left(\frac{1}{2}-1\right)} du$$

Using the definition of Gamma function, we have

$$F\left\{e^{-\left(\frac{x^2}{2}\right)}\right\} = \frac{1}{\sqrt{\pi}} e^{-\left(\frac{p^2}{2}\right)} \Gamma\left(\frac{1}{2}\right)$$

Since $\Gamma\left(\frac{1}{2}\right) = \sqrt{\pi}$, so we have

$$F\left\{e^{-\left(\frac{x^2}{2}\right)}\right\} = \frac{1}{\sqrt{\pi}} e^{-\left(\frac{p^2}{2}\right)} \sqrt{\pi} = e^{-\left(\frac{p^2}{2}\right)}$$

which shows that the Fourier transform of $e^{-\left(\frac{x^2}{2}\right)}$ is reciprocal.

**Example: 3** Find the Fourier transform of

$$F(x) = \begin{cases} 1 - x^2, & |x| \leq 1 \\ 0, & |x| > 1 \end{cases}$$

Hence evaluate $\int_0^\infty \left(\frac{x\cos x - \sin x}{x^3}\right) \cos\frac{x}{2} dx$.

**Solution:** By the definition of Fourier transform, we have

$$F\{F(x)\} = \int_{-\infty}^{\infty} F(x)e^{ipx}\,dx$$

$$\Rightarrow F\{F(x)\} = \int_{-\infty}^{-1} F(x)e^{ipx}\,dx + \int_{-1}^{1} F(x)e^{ipx}\,dx + \int_{1}^{\infty} F(x)e^{ipx}\,dx$$

By the given definition of $F(x)$, we have

$$F\{F(x)\} = \int_{-\infty}^{-1} 0 \cdot e^{ipx}\,dx + \int_{-1}^{1}(1-x^2) \cdot e^{ipx}\,dx + \int_{1}^{\infty} 0 \cdot e^{ipx}\,dx$$

$$\Rightarrow F\{F(x)\} = \int_{-1}^{1}(1-x^2)e^{ipx}\,dx$$

$$\Rightarrow F\{F(x)\} = \left[(1-x^2)\frac{e^{ipx}}{ip}\right]_{-1}^{1} - \int_{-1}^{1}(-2x)\frac{e^{ipx}}{ip}\,dx$$

$$\Rightarrow F\{F(x)\} = \frac{2}{ip}\left[x\frac{e^{ipx}}{ip}\right]_{-1}^{1} - \frac{2}{ip}\int_{-1}^{1} 1 \cdot \frac{e^{ipx}}{ip}\,dx$$

$$\Rightarrow F\{F(x)\} = -\frac{2}{p^2}\left[e^{ip}+e^{-ip}\right] + \frac{2}{p^2}\left[\frac{e^{ipx}}{ip}\right]_{-1}^{1}$$

$$\Rightarrow F\{F(x)\} = -\frac{4\cos p}{p^2} + \frac{2}{ip^3}\left[e^{ip}-e^{-ip}\right]$$

$$\Rightarrow F\{F(x)\} = -\frac{4\cos p}{p^2} + \frac{4\sin p}{p^3} = -\frac{4}{p^3}(p\cos p - \sin p)$$

By the inverse Fourier transform, we have

$$F^{-1}\{f(p)\} = \frac{1}{2\pi}\int_{-\infty}^{\infty} f(p)e^{-ipx}\, dp = F(x)$$

$$\Rightarrow F(x) = \frac{1}{2\pi}\int_{-\infty}^{\infty} e^{-ipx}\left[-\frac{4}{p^3}(p\cos p - \sin p)\right] dp$$

$$\Rightarrow F(x) = \begin{cases} 1-x^2, & |x| \le 1 \\ 0, & |x| > 1 \end{cases} = -\frac{2}{\pi}\int_{-\infty}^{\infty} e^{-ipx}\left[\frac{1}{p^3}(p\cos p - \sin p)\right] dp$$

Putting $x = \frac{1}{2}$, we have

$$-\frac{2}{\pi}\int_{-\infty}^{\infty} e^{-i\left(\frac{p}{2}\right)}\left[\frac{1}{p^3}(p\cos p - \sin p)\right] dp = 1 - \left(\frac{1}{2}\right)^2 = \frac{3}{4}$$

$$\Rightarrow \int_{-\infty}^{\infty}\left(\cos\frac{p}{2} - i\sin\frac{p}{2}\right)\left[\frac{1}{p^3}(p\cos p - \sin p)\right] dp = -\frac{3\pi}{8}$$

Equating the real parts on both sides, we have

$$\int_{-\infty}^{\infty} \cos\frac{p}{2}\left[\frac{1}{p^3}(p\cos p - \sin p)\right] dp = -\frac{3\pi}{8}$$

Since the integrand namely $\cos\frac{p}{2}\left[\frac{1}{p^3}(p\cos p - \sin p)\right]$ is an even function in the interval $(-\infty, \infty)$, so we have

$$2\int_{0}^{\infty} \cos\frac{p}{2}\left[\frac{1}{p^3}(p\cos p - \sin p)\right] dp = -\frac{3\pi}{8}$$

$$\Rightarrow \int_0^\infty \cos\frac{p}{2}\left[\frac{(p\cos p - \sin p)}{p^3}\right] dp = -\frac{3\pi}{16}$$

By replacing the dummy variable $p$ by $x$, we have

$$\int_0^\infty \left(\frac{x\cos x - \sin x}{x^3}\right)\cos\frac{x}{2} dx = -\frac{3\pi}{16}$$

**Example: 4** Find the Fourier transform of

$$F(x) = \begin{cases} e^{i\beta x}, & a < x < b \\ 0, & otherwise \end{cases}$$

**Solution:** By the definition of Fourier transform, we have

$$F\{F(x)\} = \int_{-\infty}^{\infty} F(x)e^{ipx} dx$$

$$\Rightarrow F\{F(x)\} = \int_{-\infty}^{a} F(x)e^{ipx} dx + \int_{a}^{b} F(x)e^{ipx} dx + \int_{b}^{\infty} F(x)e^{ipx} dx$$

By the given definition of $F(x)$, we have

$$F\{F(x)\} = \int_{-\infty}^{a} 0 \cdot e^{ipx} dx + \int_{a}^{b} e^{i\beta x} \cdot e^{ipx} dx + \int_{b}^{\infty} 0 \cdot e^{ipx} dx$$

$$\Rightarrow F\{F(x)\} = \int_{a}^{b} e^{i\beta x} \cdot e^{ipx} dx = \int_{a}^{b} e^{i(\beta+p)x} dx$$

$$\Rightarrow F\{F(x)\} = \left[\frac{e^{i(\beta+p)x}}{i(\beta+p)}\right]_a^b$$

$$\Rightarrow F\{F(x)\} = \left[\frac{e^{i(\beta+p)b} - e^{i(\beta+p)a}}{i(\beta+p)}\right]$$

**Example: 5** Find the Fourier transform of $F(x) = e^{-|x|}$.

**Solution:** Here $F(x) = e^{-|x|} = \begin{cases} e^x, & x < 0 \\ e^{-x}, & x > 0 \end{cases}$

By the definition of Fourier transform, we have

$$F\{F(x)\} = \int_{-\infty}^{\infty} F(x)e^{ipx}\, dx$$

$$\Rightarrow F\{F(x)\} = \int_{-\infty}^{0} F(x)e^{ipx}\, dx + \int_{0}^{\infty} F(x)e^{ipx}\, dx$$

By the given definition of $F(x)$, we have

$$F\{F(x)\} = \int_{-\infty}^{0} e^x \cdot e^{ipx}\, dx + \int_{0}^{\infty} e^{-x} \cdot e^{ipx}\, dx$$

$$\Rightarrow F\{F(x)\} = \int_{-\infty}^{0} e^{x(1+ip)}\, dx + \int_{0}^{\infty} e^{-x(1-ip)}\, dx$$

$$\Rightarrow F\{F(x)\} = \left[\frac{e^{x(1+ip)}}{(1+ip)}\right]_{-\infty}^{0} + \left[\frac{e^{-x(1-ip)}}{-(1-ip)}\right]_{0}^{\infty}$$

$$\Rightarrow F\{F(x)\} = \left[\frac{1}{(1+ip)}\right] + \left[\frac{1}{(1-ip)}\right] = \frac{2}{1+p^2}$$

**Example: 6** Find the Fourier transform of $F(x) = \begin{cases} 1, & |x| \leq \frac{a}{2} \\ 0, & otherwise \end{cases}$

**Solution:** By the definition of Fourier transform, we have

$$F\{F(x)\} = \int_{-\infty}^{\infty} F(x)e^{ipx}\, dx$$

$$\Rightarrow F\{F(x)\} = \int_{-\infty}^{-\frac{a}{2}} F(x)e^{ipx}\, dx + \int_{-\frac{a}{2}}^{\frac{a}{2}} F(x)e^{ipx}\, dx + \int_{\frac{a}{2}}^{\infty} F(x)e^{ipx}\, dx$$

By the given definition of $F(x)$, we have

$$F\{F(x)\} = \int_{-\infty}^{-\frac{a}{2}} 0.e^{ipx}\, dx + \int_{-\frac{a}{2}}^{\frac{a}{2}} 1.e^{ipx}\, dx + \int_{\frac{a}{2}}^{\infty} 0.e^{ipx}\, dx$$

$$\Rightarrow F\{F(x)\} = \int_{-\frac{a}{2}}^{\frac{a}{2}} e^{ipx}\, dx$$

$$\Rightarrow F\{F(x)\} = \left[\frac{e^{ipx}}{ip}\right]_{-\frac{a}{2}}^{\frac{a}{2}}$$

$$\Rightarrow F\{F(x)\} = \left[\frac{e^{i\left(\frac{a}{2}\right)p} - e^{-i\left(\frac{a}{2}\right)p}}{ip}\right] = 2\left[\frac{\sin\left(\frac{ap}{2}\right)}{p}\right]$$

**Example: 7** Find the Fourier transform of $F(x) = \begin{cases} -1, & x < 0 \\ 1, & x > 0 \end{cases}$.

**Solution:** Here $F(x) = \begin{cases} -1, & x < 0 \\ 1, & x > 0 \end{cases}$

By the definition of Fourier transform, we have

$$F\{F(x)\} = \int_{-\infty}^{\infty} F(x) e^{ipx} \, dx$$

$$\Rightarrow F\{F(x)\} = \int_{-\infty}^{0} F(x) e^{ipx} \, dx + \int_{0}^{\infty} F(x) e^{ipx} \, dx$$

By the given definition of $F(x)$, we have

$$F\{F(x)\} = \int_{-\infty}^{0} (-1) \cdot e^{ipx} \, dx + \int_{0}^{\infty} 1 \cdot e^{ipx} \, dx$$

$$\Rightarrow F\{F(x)\} = -\int_{-\infty}^{0} e^{ipx} \, dx + \int_{0}^{\infty} e^{ipx} \, dx$$

$$\Rightarrow F\{F(x)\} = -\left[\frac{e^{ipx}}{ip}\right]_{-\infty}^{0} + \left[\frac{e^{ipx}}{ip}\right]_{0}^{\infty}$$

$$\Rightarrow F\{F(x)\} = -\left[\frac{1}{ip} - 0\right] + \left[0 - \frac{1}{ip}\right] = -\left(\frac{2}{ip}\right)$$

**Example: 8** Find the Fourier transform of $F(x) = \begin{cases} 1, & x < 0 \\ -1, & x > 0 \end{cases}$.

21

**Solution:** Here $F(x) = \begin{cases} 1, & x < 0 \\ -1, & x > 0 \end{cases}$

By the definition of Fourier transform, we have

$$F\{F(x)\} = \int_{-\infty}^{\infty} F(x) e^{ipx} \, dx$$

$$\Rightarrow F\{F(x)\} = \int_{-\infty}^{0} F(x) e^{ipx} \, dx + \int_{0}^{\infty} F(x) e^{ipx} \, dx$$

By the given definition of $F(x)$, we have

$$F\{F(x)\} = \int_{-\infty}^{0} 1 \cdot e^{ipx} \, dx + \int_{0}^{\infty} (-1) \cdot e^{ipx} \, dx$$

$$\Rightarrow F\{F(x)\} = \int_{-\infty}^{0} e^{ipx} \, dx - \int_{0}^{\infty} e^{ipx} \, dx$$

$$\Rightarrow F\{F(x)\} = \left[\frac{e^{ipx}}{ip}\right]_{-\infty}^{0} - \left[\frac{e^{ipx}}{ip}\right]_{0}^{\infty}$$

$$\Rightarrow F\{F(x)\} = \left[\frac{1}{ip} - 0\right] - \left[0 - \frac{1}{ip}\right] = \left(\frac{2}{ip}\right)$$

**Example: 9** Find the Fourier transform of $F(x) = \begin{cases} x, & |x| < a \\ 0, & |x| > a \end{cases}$

**Solution:** Here $F(x) = \begin{cases} x, & |x| < a \\ 0, & |x| > a \end{cases}$

By the definition of Fourier transform, we have

$$F\{F(x)\} = \int_{-\infty}^{\infty} F(x)e^{ipx}\ dx$$

$$\Rightarrow F\{F(x)\} = \int_{-\infty}^{-a} F(x)e^{ipx}\ dx + \int_{-a}^{a} F(x)e^{ipx}\ dx + \int_{a}^{\infty} F(x)e^{ipx}\ dx$$

By the given definition of $F(x)$, we have

$$F\{F(x)\} = \int_{-\infty}^{-a} 0.e^{ipx}\ dx + \int_{-a}^{a} x.e^{ipx}\ dx + \int_{a}^{\infty} 0.e^{ipx}\ dx$$

$$\Rightarrow F\{F(x)\} = \int_{-a}^{a} xe^{ipx}\ dx$$

$$\Rightarrow F\{F(x)\} = \left[x\frac{e^{ipx}}{ip}\right]_{-a}^{a} - \left[\frac{e^{ipx}}{(ip)^2}\right]_{-a}^{a}$$

$$\Rightarrow F\{F(x)\} = \left[\frac{ae^{ipa} + ae^{-ipa}}{ip}\right] + \frac{1}{p^2}\left[e^{ipa} - e^{-ipa}\right]$$

$$\Rightarrow F\{F(x)\} = \left(\frac{2a\cos pa}{ip}\right) + \frac{2i\sin pa}{p^2}$$

$$\Rightarrow F\{F(x)\} = -\left(\frac{2ia\cos pa}{p}\right) + \frac{2i\sin pa}{p^2}$$

$$\Rightarrow F\{F(x)\} = \frac{2i(\sin pa - ap\cos ap)}{p^2}$$

**Example: 10** Find the Fourier transform of $F(x) = \begin{cases} 1, & -2 < x < -1 \\ 2, & -1 < x < 1 \\ 1, & 1 < x < 2 \\ 0, & otherwise \end{cases}$

**Solution:** Here $F(x) = \begin{cases} 1, & -2 < x < -1 \\ 2, & -1 < x < 1 \\ 1, & 1 < x < 2 \\ 0, & otherwise \end{cases}$

By the definition of Fourier transform, we have

$$F\{F(x)\} = \int_{-\infty}^{\infty} F(x) e^{ipx} \, dx$$

$$\Rightarrow F\{F(x)\} = \left[ \int_{-\infty}^{-2} F(x) e^{ipx} \, dx + \int_{-2}^{-1} F(x) e^{ipx} \, dx + \int_{-1}^{1} F(x) e^{ipx} \, dx \right. \\ \left. + \int_{1}^{2} F(x) e^{ipx} \, dx + \int_{2}^{\infty} F(x) e^{ipx} \, dx \right]$$

By the given definition of $F(x)$, we have

$$F\{F(x)\} = \left[ \int_{-\infty}^{-2} 0 \cdot e^{ipx} \, dx + \int_{-2}^{-1} 1 \cdot e^{ipx} \, dx + \int_{-1}^{1} 2 \cdot e^{ipx} \, dx \right. \\ \left. + \int_{1}^{2} 1 \cdot e^{ipx} \, dx + \int_{2}^{\infty} 0 \cdot e^{ipx} \, dx \right]$$

$$\Rightarrow F\{F(x)\} = \int_{-2}^{-1} e^{ipx} \, dx + 2 \int_{-1}^{1} e^{ipx} \, dx + \int_{1}^{2} e^{ipx} \, dx$$

$$\Rightarrow F\{F(x)\} = \left[ \frac{e^{ipx}}{ip} \right]_{-2}^{-1} + 2 \left[ \frac{e^{ipx}}{ip} \right]_{-1}^{1} + \left[ \frac{e^{ipx}}{ip} \right]_{1}^{2}$$

$$\Rightarrow F\{F(x)\} = \left[\frac{e^{-ip} - e^{-2ip}}{ip}\right] + 2\left[\frac{e^{ip} - e^{-ip}}{ip}\right] + \left[\frac{e^{2ip} - e^{ip}}{ip}\right]$$

$$\Rightarrow F\{F(x)\} = \left[\frac{e^{-ip} - e^{-2ip} + 2e^{ip} - 2e^{-ip} + e^{2ip} - e^{ip}}{ip}\right]$$

$$\Rightarrow F\{F(x)\} = \left[\frac{e^{ip} - e^{-ip} + e^{2ip} - e^{-2ip}}{ip}\right]$$

$$\Rightarrow F\{F(x)\} = \frac{(2i\sin p + 2i\sin 2p)}{ip} = \frac{2(\sin p + \sin 2p)}{p}$$

**Example: 11** Find the Fourier transform of $F(x) = \begin{cases} \frac{1}{2a}, & |x| \leq a \\ 0, & |x| > a \end{cases}$

**Solution:** Here $F(x) = \begin{cases} \frac{1}{2a}, & |x| \leq a \\ 0, & |x| > a \end{cases}$

By the definition of Fourier transform, we have

$$F\{F(x)\} = \int_{-\infty}^{\infty} F(x) e^{ipx} \, dx$$

$$\Rightarrow F\{F(x)\} = \int_{-\infty}^{-a} F(x) e^{ipx} \, dx + \int_{-a}^{a} F(x) e^{ipx} \, dx + \int_{a}^{\infty} F(x) e^{ipx} \, dx$$

By the given definition of $F(x)$, we have

$$F\{F(x)\} = \int_{-\infty}^{-a} 0 \cdot e^{ipx} \, dx + \int_{-a}^{a} \frac{1}{2a} \cdot e^{ipx} \, dx + \int_{a}^{\infty} 0 \cdot e^{ipx} \, dx$$

$$\Rightarrow F\{F(x)\} = \frac{1}{2a} \int_{-a}^{a} e^{ipx} \, dx$$

$$\Rightarrow F\{F(x)\} = \frac{1}{2a} \left[ \frac{e^{ipx}}{ip} \right]_{-a}^{a}$$

$$\Rightarrow F\{F(x)\} = \left[ \frac{e^{ipa} - e^{-ipa}}{2aip} \right]$$

$$\Rightarrow F\{F(x)\} = \left[ \frac{sinpa}{ap} \right]$$

## Exercise

1. Find the Fourier transform of the function

$$F(x) = \begin{cases} \lambda, & 0 < x < a \\ 0, & otherwise \end{cases}$$

Ans: $\frac{\lambda}{ip}\left[e^{ipa} - 1\right]$

2. Find the Fourier transform of the function

$$F(x) = \begin{cases} e^x, & -a < x < a \\ 0, & otherwise \end{cases}$$

Ans: $\frac{1}{(ip+1)}\left[e^{(1+ip)a} - e^{-(1+ip)a}\right]$

3. Find the Fourier transform of the function

$$F(x) = \begin{cases} 5x, & 0 < x < 3 \\ 0, & otherwise \end{cases}$$

Ans: $\frac{15}{(ip)}e^{3ip} + \frac{5}{p^2}\left[e^{3ip} - 1\right]$

4. Find the Fourier transform of the function

$$F(x) = \begin{cases} 4, & 0 < x < 2 \\ 0, & \text{otherwise} \end{cases}$$

Ans: $\frac{4}{(ip)}\left[e^{2ip} - 1\right]$

5. Find the Fourier transform of the function

$$F(x) = \begin{cases} 1, & 3 < x < 9 \\ 0, & \text{otherwise} \end{cases}$$

Ans: $\frac{1}{(ip)}\left[e^{9ip} - e^{3ip}\right]$

6. Find the Fourier transform of the function

$$F(x) = \begin{cases} 2x, & 0 < x < 7 \\ 0, & \text{otherwise} \end{cases}$$

Ans: $\frac{14}{(ip)}e^{7ip} + \frac{2}{p^2}\left[e^{7ip} - 1\right]$

7. Find the Fourier transform of the function

$$F(x) = e^{-a|x|}, a > 0$$

Ans: $\left(\frac{2a}{p^2 + a^2}\right)$

8. Find the Fourier transform of the function

$$F(x) = \begin{cases} \cos ax, & |x| < 1 \\ 0, & |x| > 1 \end{cases}$$

Ans: $\left[\frac{\sin(a+p)}{a+p} + \frac{\sin(a-p)}{a-p}\right]$

9. Find the Fourier transform of the function

$$F(x) = \begin{cases} 0, & x < a \\ 1, & a < x < b \\ 0, & x > b \end{cases}$$

Ans: $\left[\dfrac{e^{ipb}}{ip} - \dfrac{e^{ipa}}{ip}\right]$

10. Find the Fourier transform of the function

$$F(x) = \begin{cases} x^2, & |x| < a \\ 0, & |x| > a \end{cases}$$

Ans: $2\left[\dfrac{a^2 \sin ap}{p} + \dfrac{2a\cos ap}{p^2} - \dfrac{2\sin pa}{p^3}\right]$

11. Find the Fourier transform of the function

$$F(x) = \begin{cases} e^{-3x}, & x > 0 \\ e^{2x}, & x < 0 \end{cases}$$

Ans: $\left[\dfrac{1}{2+ip} + \dfrac{1}{3-ip}\right]$

12. Find the Fourier transform of the function

$$F(x) = \cos x \, e^{-|x|}.$$

Ans: $\left[\dfrac{1}{1+(p+1)^2} + \dfrac{1}{1+(p-1)^2}\right]$

13. State and prove the convolution theorem for the Fourier transform. Verify this theorem for the function $F(x) = e^{-x}$ and $G(x) = \sin x$.

# Chapter-2

## FOURIER SINE TRANSFORM

**Introduction:** In this chapter, we shall discuss the Fourier sine transform, inverse Fourier sine transform, properties of Fourier sine transform with numerical problems.

**Fourier Sine Transform:** The Fourier sine transform of $F(x)$, denoted by $F_s\{F(x)\}$, is defined by

$$F_s\{F(x)\} = \int_0^\infty F(x) \sin px\, dx = f_s(p)$$

**Inverse Fourier Sine Transform:** The inverse Fourier sine transform of $f_s(p)$, denoted by $F_s^{-1}\{f(p)\}$, is defined by

$$F_s^{-1}\{f_s(p)\} = \frac{2}{\pi}\int_0^\infty f_s(p) \sin px\, dp = F(x)$$

**Alternative Definitions of Fourier Sine Transform**

**Definition: 1**

**Fourier Sine Transform:** The Fourier sine transform of $F(x)$, denoted by $F_s\{F(x)\}$, is defined by

$$F_s\{F(x)\} = \frac{2}{\pi}\int_0^\infty F(x)sinpxdx = f_s(p)$$

**Inverse Fourier Sine Transform:** The inverse Fourier sine transform of $f_s(p)$, denoted by $F_s^{-1}\{f(p)\}$, is defined by

$$F_s^{-1}\{f_s(p)\} = \int_0^\infty f_s(p)sinpxdp = F(x)$$

**Definition: 2**

**Fourier Sine Transform:** The Fourier sine transform of $F(x)$, denoted by $F_s\{F(x)\}$, is defined by

$$F_s\{F(x)\} = \sqrt{\frac{2}{\pi}}\int_0^\infty F(x)sinpxdx = f_s(p)$$

**Inverse Fourier Sine Transform:** The inverse Fourier sine transform of $f_s(p)$, denoted by $F_s^{-1}\{f(p)\}$, is defined by

$$F_s^{-1}\{f_s(p)\} = \sqrt{\frac{2}{\pi}}\int_0^\infty f_s(p)sinpxdp = F(x)$$

**Properties of Fourier Sine Transform**

1. **Linearity Property:** If $F_s\{F(x)\} = f_s(p)$ and $F_s\{G(x)\} = g_s(p)$ then

$$F_s\{aF(x) + bG(x)\} = aF_s\{F(x)\} + bF_s\{G(x)\} = af_s(p) + bg_s(p)$$

where $a$ and $b$ are any constants.

**Proof:** By the definition of Fourier sine transform, we have

$$F_s\{F(x)\} = \int_0^\infty F(x)\sin px\, dx$$

$$\Rightarrow F_s\{aF(x) + bG(x)\} = \int_0^\infty [aF(x) + bG(x)]\sin px\, dx$$

$$\Rightarrow F_s\{aF(x) + bG(x)\} = \int_0^\infty [aF(x)]\sin px\, dx + \int_0^\infty [bG(x)]\sin px\, dx$$

$$\Rightarrow F_s\{aF(x) + bG(x)\} = a\int_0^\infty F(x)\sin px\, dx + b\int_0^\infty G(x)\sin px\, dx$$

$$\Rightarrow F_s\{aF(x) + bG(x)\} = aF_s\{F(x)\} + bF_s\{G(x)\} = af_s(p) + bg_s(p)$$

2. **Change of Scale Property or Damping Property:** If $F_s\{F(x)\} = f_s(p)$ then $F_s\{F(ax)\} = \frac{1}{a}f_s\left(\frac{p}{a}\right), a \neq 0$

**Proof:** By the definition of Fourier sine transform, we have

$$F_s\{F(x)\} = \int_0^\infty F(x)\sin px\, dx = f_s(p)$$

$$\Rightarrow F_s\{F(ax)\} = \int_0^\infty F(ax)\sin px\, dx$$

Put $ax = t \Rightarrow dx = \frac{dt}{a}$ in R.H.S. of above equation, we have

$$F_s\{F(ax)\} = \int_0^\infty \sin\left(\frac{p}{a}t\right) F(t)\frac{dt}{a} = \frac{1}{a} f_s\left(\frac{p}{a}\right), a \neq 0$$

**Example: 1** Find the Fourier sine transform of $F(x) = e^{-ax}, a > 0$. Hence evaluate $\int_0^\infty \left(\frac{p \sin px}{a^2+p^2}\right) dp$.

**Solution:** By the definition of Fourier sine transform of $F(x)$, we have

$$F_s\{F(x)\} = \int_0^\infty F(x)\sin px\, dx$$

$$\Rightarrow F_s\{e^{-ax}\} = \int_0^\infty e^{-ax} \sin px\, dx$$

$$\Rightarrow F_s\{e^{-ax}\} = \left[\frac{e^{-ax}}{a^2+p^2}(-a\sin px - p\cos px)\right]_0^\infty$$

$$\Rightarrow F_s\{e^{-ax}\} = \left[0 - \frac{1}{a^2+p^2}(-p)\right] = \frac{p}{a^2+p^2} = f_s(p)$$

Taking the inverse Fourier sine transform of both sides of above equation, we have

$$F_s^{-1}\{f_s(p)\} = \frac{2}{\pi}\int_0^\infty f_s(p)\sin px\, dp = F(x)$$

$$\Rightarrow e^{-ax} = \frac{2}{\pi}\int_0^\infty \frac{p}{a^2+p^2}\sin px\, dp$$

$$\Rightarrow \int_0^\infty \frac{p\sin px}{a^2+p^2} dp = \frac{\pi}{2}e^{-ax}$$

**Example: 2** Find the Fourier sine transform of $F(x) = e^{-|x|}$. Hence show that

$\int_0^\infty \left(\frac{x \sin ax}{1+x^2}\right) dx = \frac{\pi}{2} e^{-a}, a > 0$.

**Solution:** The variable $x$ is positive in the interval $(0, \infty)$ so that $|x| = x$ for $(0, \infty)$.

By the definition of Fourier sine transform of $F(x)$, we have

$$F_s\{F(x)\} = \int_0^\infty F(x) \sin px \, dx$$

$$\Rightarrow F_s\{e^{-|x|}\} = F_s\{e^{-x}\} = \int_0^\infty e^{-x} \sin px \, dx$$

$$\Rightarrow F_s\{e^{-x}\} = \left[\frac{e^{-x}}{1+p^2}(-\sin px - p\cos px)\right]_0^\infty$$

$$\Rightarrow F_s\{e^{-x}\} = \left[0 - \frac{1}{1+p^2}(-p)\right] = \frac{p}{1+p^2} = f_s(p)$$

Taking the inverse Fourier sine transform of both sides of above equation, we have

$$F_s^{-1}\{f_s(p)\} = \frac{2}{\pi} \int_0^\infty f_s(p) \sin px \, dp = F(x)$$

$$\Rightarrow e^{-x} = \frac{2}{\pi} \int_0^\infty \frac{p}{1+p^2} \sin px \, dp$$

Replacing $x$ by $a$ in above equation, we have

$$\Rightarrow \int_0^\infty \frac{p\,sinap}{1+p^2}\,dp = \frac{\pi}{2}e^{-a}$$

By changing the dummy variable $p$ by $x$, we have

$$\int_0^\infty \left(\frac{xsinax}{1+x^2}\right)dx = \frac{\pi}{2}e^{-a}, a > 0$$

**Example: 3** Find the Fourier sine transform of $F(x) = \frac{e^{-ax}}{x}$.

**Solution:** By the definition of Fourier sine transform of $F(x)$, we have

$$F_s\{F(x)\} = \int_0^\infty F(x)sinpx\,dx$$

$$\Rightarrow F_s\left\{\frac{e^{-ax}}{x}\right\} = \int_0^\infty \frac{e^{-ax}}{x}sinpx\,dx = I (Let)$$

Differentiating both sides of above equation with respect to $p$, we have

$$\frac{dI}{dp} = \frac{d}{dp}\int_0^\infty \frac{e^{-ax}}{x}sinpx\,dx$$

$$\Rightarrow \frac{dI}{dp} = \int_0^\infty \frac{\partial}{\partial p}\left(\frac{e^{-ax}}{x}sinpx\right)dx$$

$$\Rightarrow \frac{dI}{dp} = \int_0^\infty \left(\frac{e^{-ax}}{x}\right)\frac{\partial}{\partial p}(sinpx)\,dx$$

$$\Rightarrow \frac{dI}{dp} = \int_0^\infty e^{-ax} \cos px \, dx$$

$$\Rightarrow \frac{dI}{dp} = \left[ \frac{e^{-ax}}{a^2 + p^2} (-a\cos px + p\sin px) \right]_0^\infty$$

$$\Rightarrow \frac{dI}{dp} = \left[ 0 - \frac{1}{a^2 + p^2}(-a) \right] = \frac{a}{a^2 + p^2}$$

On integration, we have

$$I = \tan^{-1}\left(\frac{p}{a}\right) + c$$

Since $I = 0$ when $p = 0$ so using this in above equation, we have

$$c = 0$$

Hence $I = F_s\left\{\frac{e^{-ax}}{x}\right\} = \tan^{-1}\left(\frac{p}{a}\right)$.

**Example: 4** Find the Fourier sine transform of the function

$$F(x) = \begin{cases} 1, & 0 \le x < a \\ 0, & x > a \end{cases}$$

**Solution:** By the definition of Fourier sine transform of $F(x)$, we have

$$F_s\{F(x)\} = \int_0^\infty F(x) \sin px \, dx = f_s(p)$$

$$\Rightarrow F_s\{F(x)\} = \int_0^a F(x)sinpx\,dx + \int_a^\infty F(x)sinpx\,dx$$

By the given definition of $F(x)$, we have

$$F_s\{F(x)\} = \int_0^a 1.sinpx\,dx + \int_a^\infty 0.sinpx\,dx$$

$$\Rightarrow F_s\{F(x)\} = \int_0^a sinpx\,dx$$

$$\Rightarrow F_s\{F(x)\} = \left[\frac{-cospx}{p}\right]_0^a$$

$$\Rightarrow F_s\{F(x)\} = -\left[\frac{cospa-1}{p}\right] = \left[\frac{1-cosap}{p}\right]$$

**Example: 5** Find the Fourier sine transform of $F(x) = \begin{cases} x, & 0 < x < 1 \\ 2-x, & 1 < x < 2 \\ 0, & x > 2 \end{cases}$

**Solution:** By the definition of Fourier sine transform of $F(x)$, we have

$$F_s\{F(x)\} = \int_0^\infty F(x)sinpx\,dx = f_s(p)$$

$$\Rightarrow F_s\{F(x)\} = \int_0^1 F(x)sinpx\,dx + \int_1^2 F(x)sinpx\,dx + \int_2^\infty F(x)sinpx\,dx$$

$$\Rightarrow F_s\{F(x)\} = \int_0^1 xsinpx\,dx + \int_1^2 (2-x)sinpx\,dx + \int_2^\infty 0.sinpx\,dx$$

$$\Rightarrow F_s\{F(x)\} = \left[-x\frac{cospx}{p}\right]_0^1 - \left[-\frac{sinpx}{p^2}\right]_0^1 + \left[-(2-x)\frac{cospx}{p}\right]_1^2 - \left[\frac{sinpx}{p^2}\right]_1^2$$

$$\Rightarrow F_s\{F(x)\} = -\frac{cosp}{p} + \left(\frac{sinp}{p^2}\right) + \frac{cosp}{p} - \left(\frac{sin2p - sinp}{p^2}\right)$$

$$\Rightarrow F_s\{F(x)\} = \left(\frac{2sinp - sin2p}{p^2}\right)$$

**Example: 6** Find the Fourier sine transform of $F(x) = \begin{cases} 0, & 0 < x < a \\ x, & a \le x \le b \\ 0, & x > b \end{cases}$

**Solution:** By the definition of Fourier sine transform of $F(x)$, we have

$$F_s\{F(x)\} = \int_0^\infty F(x) sinpx\, dx = f_s(p)$$

$$\Rightarrow F_s\{F(x)\} = \int_0^a F(x) sinpx\, dx + \int_a^b F(x) sinpx\, dx + \int_b^\infty F(x) sinpx\, dx$$

$$\Rightarrow F_s\{F(x)\} = \int_0^a 0.sinpx\, dx + \int_a^b x sinpx\, dx + \int_b^\infty 0.sinpx\, dx$$

$$\Rightarrow F_s\{F(x)\} = \int_a^b x sinpx\, dx$$

$$\Rightarrow F_s\{F(x)\} = \left[-x\frac{cospx}{p}\right]_a^b + \left[\frac{sinpx}{p^2}\right]_a^b$$

$$\Rightarrow F_s\{F(x)\} = -\left[\frac{b\cos bp - a\cos ap}{p}\right] + \left[\frac{\sin pb - \sin pa}{p^2}\right]$$

$$\Rightarrow F_s\{F(x)\} = \left[\frac{a\cos ap - b\cos bp}{p}\right] + \left[\frac{\sin pb - \sin pa}{p^2}\right]$$

## Exercise

1. Find the Fourier sine transform of the function $F(x) = e^{-7x}$.

   Ans: $\left(\frac{p}{p^2+49}\right)$

2. Find the Fourier sine transform of the function $F(x) = 2e^{-5x} + 5e^{-2x}$.

   Ans: $\left(\frac{2p}{p^2+25}\right) + \left(\frac{5p}{p^2+4}\right)$

3. Find the Fourier sine transform of the function $F(x) = x^{m-1}, m > 0$.

   Ans: $\left(\frac{\Gamma(m)}{p^m}\right) \sin\frac{m\pi}{2}$

4. Find the Fourier sine transform of the function $F(x) = \frac{e^{-ax} - e^{-bx}}{x}$.

   Ans: $\tan^{-1}\frac{p}{a} - \tan^{-1}\frac{p}{b}$

5. Find the Fourier sine transform of the function $F(x) = \frac{1}{\sqrt{x}}$.

   Ans: $\sqrt{\frac{\pi}{2p}}$

6. Find the Fourier sine transform of the function $F(x) = \cosh x - \sinh x$.

   Ans: $\left(\frac{p}{p^2+1}\right)$

# Chapter-3

## FOURIER COSINE TRANSFORM

**Introduction:** In this chapter, we shall discuss the Fourier cosine transform, inverse Fourier cosine transform, properties of Fourier cosine transform with numerical problems.

**Fourier Cosine Transform:** The Fourier cosine transform of $F(x)$, denoted by $F_c\{F(x)\}$, is defined by

$$F_c\{F(x)\} = \int_0^\infty F(x) \cos px\, dx = f_c(p)$$

**Inverse Fourier Cosine Transform:** The inverse Fourier cosine transform of $f_c(p)$, denoted by $F_c^{-1}\{f(p)\}$, is defined by

$$F_c^{-1}\{f_c(p)\} = \frac{2}{\pi}\int_0^\infty f_c(p) \cos px\, dp = F(x)$$

**Alternative Definitions of Fourier Cosine Transform:**

**Definition: 1**

**Fourier Cosine Transform:** The Fourier cosine transform of $F(x)$, denoted by $F_c\{F(x)\}$, is defined by

$$F_c\{F(x)\} = \frac{2}{\pi}\int_0^\infty F(x)\cos px\, dx = f_c(p)$$

**Inverse Fourier Cosine Transform:** The inverse Fourier cosine transform of $f_c(p)$, denoted by $F_c^{-1}\{f(p)\}$, is defined by

$$F_c^{-1}\{f_c(p)\} = \int_0^\infty f_c(p)\cos px\, dp = F(x)$$

**Definition: 2**

**Fourier Cosine Transform:** The Fourier cosine transform of $F(x)$, denoted by $F_c\{F(x)\}$, is defined by

$$F_c\{F(x)\} = \sqrt{\frac{2}{\pi}}\int_0^\infty F(x)\cos px\, dx = f_c(p)$$

**Inverse Fourier Cosine Transform:** The inverse Fourier cosine transform of $f_c(p)$, denoted by $F_c^{-1}\{f(p)\}$, is defined by

$$F_c^{-1}\{f_c(p)\} = \sqrt{\frac{2}{\pi}}\int_0^\infty f_c(p)\cos px\, dp = F(x)$$

**Properties of Fourier Cosine Transform:**

1. **Linearity Property:** If $F_c\{F(x)\} = f_c(p)$ and $F_c\{G(x)\} = g_c(p)$ then

$$F_c\{aF(x) + bG(x)\} = aF_c\{F(x)\} + bF_c\{G(x)\} = af_c(p) + bg_c(p)$$

where $a$ and $b$ are any constants.

**Proof:** By the definition of Fourier cosine transform, we have

$$F_c\{F(x)\} = \int_0^\infty F(x)\cos px\, dx$$

$$\Rightarrow F_c\{aF(x) + bG(x)\} = \int_0^\infty [aF(x) + bG(x)]\cos px\, dx$$

$$\Rightarrow F_c\{aF(x) + bG(x)\} = \int_0^\infty [aF(x)]\cos px\, dx + \int_0^\infty [bG(x)]\cos px\, dx$$

$$\Rightarrow F_c\{aF(x) + bG(x)\} = a\int_0^\infty F(x)\cos px\, dx + b\int_0^\infty G(x)\cos px\, dx$$

$$\Rightarrow F_c\{aF(x) + bG(x)\} = aF_c\{F(x)\} + bF_c\{G(x)\} = af_c(p) + bg_c(p)$$

2. **Change of Scale Property or Damping Property:** If $F_c\{F(x)\} = f_c(p)$

then $F_c\{F(ax)\} = \frac{1}{a} f_c\left(\frac{p}{a}\right), a \neq 0$

**Proof:** By the definition of Fourier cosine transform, we have

$$F_c\{F(x)\} = \int_0^\infty F(x)\cos px\, dx = f_c(p)$$

$$\Rightarrow F_c\{F(ax)\} = \int_0^\infty F(ax)\cos px\, dx$$

Put $ax = t \Rightarrow dx = \frac{dt}{a}$ in R.H.S. of above equation, we have

$$F_c\{F(ax)\} = \int_0^\infty \cos\left(\frac{p}{a}t\right)F(t)\frac{dt}{a} = \frac{1}{a}f_c\left(\frac{p}{a}\right), a \neq 0$$

**Example: 1** Find the Fourier cosine transform of $F(x) = e^{-ax}, a > 0$. Hence evaluate $\int_0^\infty \left(\frac{cospx}{a^2+p^2}\right)dp$.

**Solution:** By the definition of Fourier cosine transform, we have

$$F_c\{F(x)\} = \int_0^\infty F(x)cospx\, dx$$

$$\Rightarrow F_c\{e^{-ax}\} = \int_0^\infty e^{-ax}cospx\, dx$$

$$\Rightarrow F_c\{e^{-ax}\} = \left[\frac{e^{-ax}}{a^2+p^2}(-acospx + psinpx)\right]_0^\infty$$

$$\Rightarrow F_c\{e^{-ax}\} = \left[0 - \frac{1}{a^2+p^2}(-a)\right] = \frac{a}{a^2+p^2} = f_c(p)$$

Taking the inverse Fourier cosine transform of both sides of above equation, we have

$$F_c^{-1}\{f_c(p)\} = \frac{2}{\pi}\int_0^\infty f_c(p)cospx\, dp = F(x)$$

$$\Rightarrow e^{-ax} = \frac{2}{\pi}\int_0^\infty \frac{a}{a^2+p^2}cospx\, dp$$

$$\Rightarrow \int_0^\infty \frac{cospx}{a^2+p^2} dp = \frac{\pi}{2a} e^{-ax}$$

**Example: 2** Find the Fourier cosine transform of $F(x) = \begin{cases} x, & 0 < x < 1 \\ 2-x, & 1 < x < 2 \\ 0, & x > 2 \end{cases}$

**Solution:** By the definition of Fourier cosine transform of $F(x)$, we have

$$F_c\{F(x)\} = \int_0^\infty F(x) cospx\, dx = f_c(p)$$

$$\Rightarrow F_c\{F(x)\} = \int_0^1 F(x) cospx\, dx + \int_1^2 F(x) cospx\, dx + \int_2^\infty F(x) cospx\, dx$$

$$\Rightarrow F_c\{F(x)\} = \int_0^1 x cospx\, dx + \int_1^2 (2-x) cospx\, dx + \int_2^\infty 0 \cdot cospx\, dx$$

$$\Rightarrow F_c\{F(x)\} = \left[x \frac{sinpx}{p}\right]_0^1 - \left[-\frac{cospx}{p^2}\right]_0^1 + \left[(2-x)\frac{sinpx}{p}\right]_1^2 - \left[\frac{cospx}{p^2}\right]_1^2$$

$$\Rightarrow F_c\{F(x)\} = \frac{sinp}{p} + \left(\frac{cosp-1}{p^2}\right) - \frac{sinp}{p} - \left(\frac{cos2p-cosp}{p^2}\right)$$

$$\Rightarrow F_c\{F(x)\} = \left(\frac{2cosp - cos2p - 1}{p^2}\right)$$

**Example: 3** Find the Fourier cosine transform of the function

43

$$F(x) = \begin{cases} x, & 0 < x < \frac{1}{2} \\ 1-x, & \frac{1}{2} < x < 1 \\ 0, & x > 1 \end{cases}$$

**Solution:** By the definition of Fourier cosine transform of $F(x)$, we have

$$F_c\{F(x)\} = \int_0^\infty F(x)\cos px\, dx = f_c(p)$$

$$\Rightarrow F_c\{F(x)\} = \int_0^{\frac{1}{2}} F(x)\cos px\, dx + \int_{\frac{1}{2}}^1 F(x)\cos px\, dx + \int_1^\infty F(x)\cos px\, dx$$

By the given definition of $F(x)$, we have

$$F_c\{F(x)\} = \int_0^{\frac{1}{2}} x\cos px\, dx + \int_{\frac{1}{2}}^1 (1-x)\cos px\, dx + \int_1^\infty 0\cdot\cos px\, dx$$

$$\Rightarrow F_c\{F(x)\} = \left[x\frac{\sin px}{p}\right]_0^{\frac{1}{2}} - \left[-\frac{\cos px}{p^2}\right]_0^{\frac{1}{2}} + \left[(1-x)\frac{\sin px}{p}\right]_{\frac{1}{2}}^1 - \left[\frac{\cos px}{p^2}\right]_{\frac{1}{2}}^1$$

$$\Rightarrow F_c\{F(x)\} = \left[\frac{\sin\left(\frac{p}{2}\right)}{2p}\right] + \left[\frac{\cos\left(\frac{p}{2}\right) - 1}{p^2}\right] - \left[\frac{\sin\left(\frac{p}{2}\right)}{2p}\right] - \left[\frac{\cos p - \cos\left(\frac{p}{2}\right)}{p^2}\right]$$

$$\Rightarrow F_c\{F(x)\} = \left[\frac{2\cos\left(\frac{p}{2}\right) - \cos p - 1}{p^2}\right]$$

**Example: 4** Find the Fourier cosine transform of the function

$$F(x) = \begin{cases} cosx, & 0 < x < a \\ 0, & x > a \end{cases}$$

**Solution:** By the definition of Fourier cosine transform of $F(x)$, we have

$$F_c\{F(x)\} = \int_0^\infty F(x) cospx\, dx = f_c(p)$$

$$\Rightarrow F_c\{F(x)\} = \int_0^a F(x) cospx\, dx + \int_a^\infty F(x) cospx\, dx$$

By the given definition of $F(x)$, we have

$$F_c\{F(x)\} = \int_0^a cosx\, cospx\, dx + \int_a^\infty 0.cospx\, dx$$

$$\Rightarrow F_c\{F(x)\} = \int_0^a cosx\, cospx\, dx$$

$$\Rightarrow F_c\{F(x)\} = \frac{1}{2}\int_0^a [cos(1+p)x + cos(1-p)x]\, dx$$

$$\Rightarrow F_c\{F(x)\} = \frac{1}{2}\left[\frac{sin(1+p)x}{(1+p)} + \frac{sin(1-p)x}{(1-p)}\right]_0^a$$

$$\Rightarrow F_c\{F(x)\} = \frac{1}{2}\left[\frac{sin(1+p)a}{(1+p)} + \frac{sin(1-p)a}{(1-p)}\right]$$

## Exercise

1. Find the Fourier cosine transform of the function $F(x) = e^{-7x}$.

   Ans: $\left(\dfrac{7}{p^2+49}\right)$

2. Find the Fourier cosine transform of the function $F(x) = 2e^{-5x} + 5e^{-2x}$.

   Ans: $\left(\dfrac{10}{p^2+25}\right) + \left(\dfrac{10}{p^2+4}\right)$

3. Find the Fourier cosine transform of the function $F(x) = x^{m-1}, m > 0$.

   Ans: $\left(\dfrac{\Gamma(m)}{p^m}\right) \cos \dfrac{m\pi}{2}$

4. Find the Fourier cosine transform of the function $F(x) = \dfrac{1}{\sqrt{x}}$.

   Ans: $\sqrt{\dfrac{\pi}{2p}}$

5. Find the Fourier cosine transform of the function $F(x) = \cosh x - \sinh x$.

   Ans: $\left(\dfrac{1}{p^2+1}\right)$

6. Find the Fourier cosine transform of the function $F(x) = e^{-2x} + 4e^{-3x}$.

   Ans: $\left(\dfrac{2}{p^2+4}\right) + \left(\dfrac{12}{p^2+9}\right)$

7. Find the Fourier cosine transform of the function $F(x) = e^{-ax} \cos ax$.

   Ans: $\left[\dfrac{2a}{a^2+(p+a)^2} + \dfrac{2a}{a^2+(p-a)^2}\right]$

# Chapter-4

## FINITE FOURIER SINE TRANSFORM

**Introduction:** In this chapter, we shall discuss the finite Fourier sine transform, inverse finite Fourier sine transform with numerical problems.

**Finite Fourier Sine Transform:** The finite Fourier sine transform of $F(x)$ in the interval $(0, l)$ is defined by

$$f_s(n) = \int_0^l F(x) \sin\frac{n\pi x}{l} dx$$

where $n$ is an integer.

**Inverse Finite Fourier Sine Transform:** The function $F(x)$ is called the inverse finite Fourier sine transform of $f_s(n)$ and is given by

$$F(x) = \frac{2}{l} \sum_{n=1}^{\infty} f_s(n) \sin\frac{n\pi x}{l}$$

**Example: 1** Find the finite Fourier sine transform of $F(x) = 1$, $0 < x < \pi$.

**Solution:** By the definition of finite Fourier sine transform of $F(x)$, we have

$$f_s(n) = \int_0^l F(x) \sin\frac{n\pi x}{l} dx$$

where $n$ is an integer.

Here $F(x) = 1$ and $l = \pi$ so we have

$$f_s(n) = \int_0^\pi 1.sinnx\, dx = \left[-\frac{cosnx}{n}\right]_0^\pi$$

$$\Rightarrow f_s(n) = \left[-\frac{cosn\pi}{n} + \frac{1}{n}\right]$$

$$\Rightarrow f_s(n) = \left(\frac{1 - cosn\pi}{n}\right)$$

**Example: 2** Find the finite Fourier sine transform of $F(x) = x, 0 < x < \pi$.

**Solution:** By the definition of finite Fourier sine transform of $F(x)$, we have

$$f_s(n) = \int_0^l F(x) sin\frac{n\pi x}{l} dx$$

where $n$ is an integer.

Here $F(x) = x$ and $l = \pi$ so we have

$$f_s(n) = \int_0^\pi xsinnx\, dx = \left[-x\frac{cosnx}{n}\right]_0^\pi - \left[-\frac{sinnx}{n^2}\right]_0^\pi$$

$$\Rightarrow f_s(n) = \left[-\pi\frac{cosn\pi}{n} + 0\right] + \left[\frac{sinn\pi}{n^2} - 0\right]$$

$$\Rightarrow f_s(n) = -\left(\frac{\pi \cos n\pi}{n}\right)$$

**Example: 3** Find the finite Fourier sine transform of $F(x) = x^2, 0 < x < \pi$.

**Solution:** By the definition of finite Fourier sine transform of $F(x)$, we have

$$f_s(n) = \int_0^l F(x) \sin\frac{n\pi x}{l} dx$$

where $n$ is an integer.

Here $F(x) = x^2$ and $l = \pi$ so we have

$$f_s(n) = \int_0^\pi x^2 \sin nx \, dx = \left[-x^2 \frac{\cos nx}{n}\right]_0^\pi - \int_0^\pi 2x\left[-\frac{\cos nx}{n}\right] dx$$

$$\Rightarrow f_s(n) = \left[-\pi^2 \frac{\cos n\pi}{n} + 0\right] + \frac{2}{n}\int_0^\pi x\cos nx \, dx$$

$$\Rightarrow f_s(n) = -\left(\frac{\pi^2 \cos n\pi}{n}\right) + \frac{2}{n}\left\{\left[x\frac{\sin nx}{n}\right]_0^\pi - \left[-\frac{\cos nx}{n^2}\right]_0^\pi\right\}$$

$$\Rightarrow f_s(n) = -\left(\frac{\pi^2 \cos n\pi}{n}\right) + \frac{2}{n}\left\{\left[\pi\frac{\sin n\pi}{n} - 0\right] + \left[\frac{\cos n\pi}{n^2} - \frac{1}{n^2}\right]\right\}$$

$$\Rightarrow f_s(n) = -\left(\frac{\pi^2 \cos n\pi}{n}\right) + \frac{2}{n}\left(\frac{\cos n\pi - 1}{n^2}\right)$$

$$\Rightarrow f_s(n) = \left[\frac{(2 - n^2\pi^2)\cos n\pi - 2}{n^3}\right]$$

**Example: 4** Find the finite Fourier sine transform of $F(x) = e^x, 0 < x < 1$.

**Solution:** By the definition of finite Fourier sine transform of $F(x)$, we have

$$f_s(n) = \int_0^l F(x) \sin\frac{n\pi x}{l} dx$$

where $n$ is an integer.

Here $F(x) = e^x$ and $l = 1$ so we have

$$f_s(n) = \int_0^1 e^x \sin n\pi x \, dx = \left[\frac{e^x}{1 + n^2\pi^2}(\sin n\pi x - n\pi \cos n\pi x)\right]_0^1$$

$$\Rightarrow f_s(n) = \left[\frac{e}{1 + n^2\pi^2}(\sin n\pi - n\pi \cos n\pi) - \frac{1}{1 + n^2\pi^2}(0 - n\pi)\right]$$

$$\Rightarrow f_s(n) = \frac{n\pi}{1 + n^2\pi^2}[1 - e\cos n\pi]$$

**Example: 5** Find the finite Fourier sine transform of $F(x) = \begin{cases} x, & 0 \le x < \pi/2 \\ \pi - x, & \pi/2 < x \le \pi \end{cases}$

**Solution:** By the definition of finite Fourier sine transform of $F(x)$, we have

$$f_s(n) = \int_0^l F(x) \sin\frac{n\pi x}{l} dx$$

where $n$ is an integer.

Here $F(x) = \begin{cases} x, & 0 \le x < \pi/2 \\ \pi - x, & \pi/2 < x \le \pi \end{cases}$ and $l = \pi$ so we have

$$f_s(n) = \int_0^\pi F(x) sinnx \, dx$$

$$\Rightarrow f_s(n) = \int_0^{\pi/2} F(x) sinnx \, dx + \int_{\pi/2}^\pi F(x) sinnx \, dx$$

$$\Rightarrow f_s(n) = \int_0^{\pi/2} x sinnx \, dx + \int_{\pi/2}^\pi (\pi - x) sinnx \, dx$$

$$\Rightarrow f_s(n) = \left[-x \frac{cosnx}{n}\right]_0^{\pi/2} - \left[-\frac{sinnx}{n^2}\right]_0^{\pi/2} + \left[-(\pi - x)\frac{cosnx}{n}\right]_{\pi/2}^\pi - \left[\frac{sinnx}{n^2}\right]_{\pi/2}^\pi$$

$$\Rightarrow f_s(n) = \left\{-\frac{\pi}{2n} cos \frac{n\pi}{2}\right\} + \frac{1}{n^2}\left\{sin \frac{n\pi}{2}\right\} + \left\{\frac{\pi}{2n} cos \frac{n\pi}{2}\right\} - \frac{1}{n^2}\left\{sinn\pi - sin \frac{n\pi}{2}\right\}$$

$$\Rightarrow f_s(n) = \frac{1}{n^2}\left\{sin \frac{n\pi}{2}\right\} - \frac{1}{n^2}\left\{0 - sin \frac{n\pi}{2}\right\}$$

$$\Rightarrow f_s(n) = \frac{2}{n^2} sin \frac{n\pi}{2}$$

**Example: 6** Find the finite Fourier sine transform of $F(x) = \begin{cases} 0, & 0 \le x < \pi/2 \\ 1, & \pi/2 < x \le \pi \end{cases}$

**Solution:** By the definition of finite Fourier sine transform of $F(x)$, we have

$$f_s(n) = \int_0^l F(x) sin\frac{n\pi x}{l} dx$$

51

where $n$ is an integer.

Here $F(x) = \begin{cases} 0, & 0 \leq x < \pi/2 \\ 1, & \pi/2 < x \leq \pi \end{cases}$ and $l = \pi$ so we have

$$f_s(n) = \int_0^\pi F(x) sinnx\, dx$$

$$\Rightarrow f_s(n) = \int_0^{\pi/2} F(x) sinnx\, dx + \int_{\pi/2}^\pi F(x) sinnx\, dx$$

$$\Rightarrow f_s(n) = \int_0^{\pi/2} 0.sinnx\, dx + \int_{\pi/2}^\pi 1.sinnx\, dx$$

$$\Rightarrow f_s(n) = \left[-\frac{cosnx}{n}\right]_{\pi/2}^\pi = \frac{1}{n}\left\{cos\frac{n\pi}{2} - cosn\pi\right\}$$

**Example: 7** Find the finite Fourier sine transform of $F(x)$, where

$$F(x) = \begin{cases} 1, & 0 \leq x < \pi/2 \\ -1, & \pi/2 < x \leq \pi \end{cases}$$

**Solution:** By the definition of finite Fourier sine transform of $F(x)$, we have

$$f_s(n) = \int_0^l F(x) sin\frac{n\pi x}{l}\, dx$$

where $n$ is an integer.

Here $F(x) = \begin{cases} 1, & 0 \leq x < \pi/2 \\ -1, & \pi/2 < x \leq \pi \end{cases}$ and $l = \pi$ so we have

$$f_s(n) = \int_0^\pi F(x)\sin nx\, dx$$

$$\Rightarrow f_s(n) = \int_0^{\pi/2} F(x)\sin nx\, dx + \int_{\pi/2}^{\pi} F(x)\sin nx\, dx$$

$$\Rightarrow f_s(n) = \int_0^{\pi/2} 1.\sin nx\, dx + \int_{\pi/2}^{\pi} (-1).\sin nx\, dx$$

$$\Rightarrow f_s(n) = \int_0^{\pi/2} \sin nx\, dx - \int_{\pi/2}^{\pi} \sin nx\, dx$$

$$\Rightarrow f_s(n) = \left[-\frac{\cos nx}{n}\right]_0^{\pi/2} - \left[-\frac{\cos nx}{n}\right]_{\pi/2}^{\pi}$$

$$\Rightarrow f_s(n) = -\frac{1}{n}\left\{\cos\frac{n\pi}{2} - 1\right\} + \frac{1}{n}\left\{\cos n\pi - \cos\frac{n\pi}{2}\right\}$$

$$\Rightarrow f_s(n) = \frac{1}{n}\left\{\cos n\pi - 2\cos\frac{n\pi}{2} + 1\right\}$$

**Example: 8** Find the inverse finite Fourier sine transform $F(x)$ of

$$f_s(n) = \frac{1 - \cos n\pi}{n^2 \pi^2}, 0 < x < \pi$$

**Solution:** By the definition of inverse finite Fourier sine transform of $f_s(n)$, we have

$$F(x) = \frac{2}{l}\sum_{n=1}^{\infty} f_s(n)\sin\frac{n\pi x}{l}, 0 < x < l$$

Here $f_s(n) = \frac{1-\cos n\pi}{n^2\pi^2}$ and $l = \pi$, so we have

$$F(x) = \frac{2}{\pi}\sum_{n=1}^{\infty} f_s(n)\sin nx$$

$$\Rightarrow F(x) = \frac{2}{\pi}\sum_{n=1}^{\infty}\left(\frac{1-\cos n\pi}{n^2\pi^2}\right)\sin nx$$

$$\Rightarrow F(x) = \frac{2}{\pi}\sum_{n=1}^{\infty}\left[\frac{1-(-1)^n}{n^2\pi^2}\right]\sin nx$$

$$\Rightarrow F(x) = \frac{2}{\pi^3}\left[\frac{2}{1^2}\sin x + \frac{2}{3^2}\sin 3x + \frac{2}{5^2}\sin 5x + \cdots\cdots\right]$$

$$\Rightarrow F(x) = \frac{4}{\pi^3}\left[\sin x + \frac{1}{3^2}\sin 3x + \frac{1}{5^2}\sin 5x + \cdots\cdots\right]$$

**Example: 9** Find the inverse finite Fourier sine transform $F(x)$ of

$$f_s(n) = \frac{16(-1)^{n-1}}{n^3}, 0 < x < 8$$

**Solution:** By the definition of inverse finite Fourier sine transform of $f_s(n)$, we have

$$F(x) = \frac{2}{l}\sum_{n=1}^{\infty} f_s(n)\sin\frac{n\pi x}{l}, 0 < x < l$$

Here $f_s(n) = \frac{16(-1)^{n-1}}{n^3}$ and $l = 8$, so we have

$$F(x) = \frac{2}{8}\sum_{n=1}^{\infty} f_s(n)\sin\frac{n\pi x}{8}$$

$$\Rightarrow F(x) = \frac{2}{8}\sum_{n=1}^{\infty} \frac{16(-1)^{n-1}}{n^3}\sin\frac{n\pi x}{8}$$

$$\Rightarrow F(x) = 4\sum_{n=1}^{\infty} \frac{(-1)^{n-1}}{n^3}\sin\frac{n\pi x}{8}$$

### Exercise

1. Find the finite Fourier sine transform of the function

$$F(x) = 2x, 0 < x < 4$$

Ans: $f_s(n) = -\frac{32}{n\pi}\cos n\pi$

2. Show that the finite Fourier sine transform of the function $F(x) = \frac{x}{\pi}$, where $0 < x < \pi$ is $\frac{(-1)^{n+1}}{n}$.

3. Find the finite Fourier sine transform of the function

$$F(x) = \left(1 - \frac{x}{\pi}\right), 0 < x < \pi$$

Ans: $f_s(n) = \dfrac{1}{n}$

4. Find the finite Fourier sine transform of the function

$$F(x) = \left(\dfrac{x}{4\pi}\right), 0 < x < \pi$$

Ans: $f_s(n) = \dfrac{(-1)^{n+1}}{4n}$

5. Find the finite Fourier sine transform of the function

$$F(x) = x(\pi - x), 0 < x < \pi$$

Ans: $f_s(n) = \dfrac{2}{n^3}[1 - (-1)^n]$

6. Find the finite Fourier sine transform of the function

$$F(x) = x(\pi^2 - x^2), 0 < x < \pi$$

Ans: $f_s(n) = \dfrac{6\pi}{n^3}(-1)^{n+1}$

7. Find the finite Fourier sine transform of the function

$$F(x) = sinpx, 0 < x < \pi$$

Ans: $f_s(n) = \begin{cases} 0, & p \neq n \\ \dfrac{\pi}{2}, & p = n \end{cases}$

8. Find $F(x)$ if its finite sine transform is given by

$$f_s(n) = \dfrac{2\pi(-1)^{n-1}}{n^3}, n = 1,2,3,\ldots\ldots, \text{ where } 0 < x < 8$$

Ans: $F(x) = 4\sum_{n=1}^{\infty} \dfrac{(-1)^{n-1}}{n^3} sinnx$

# Chapter-5

# FINITE FOURIER COSINE TRANSFORM

**Introduction:** In this chapter, we shall discuss the finite Fourier cosine transform, inverse finite Fourier cosine transform with numerical problems.

**Finite Fourier Cosine Transform:** The finite Fourier cosine transform of $F(x)$ in the interval $(0, l)$ is defined by

$$f_c(n) = \int_0^l F(x) \cos\frac{n\pi x}{l} dx$$

where $n$ is an integer.

**Inverse Finite Fourier Cosine Transform:** The function $F(x)$ is called the inverse finite Fourier cosine transform of $f_c(n)$ and is given by

$$F(x) = \frac{1}{l} f_c(0) + \frac{2}{l} \sum_{n=1}^{\infty} f_c(n) \cos\frac{n\pi x}{l}$$

where $f_c(0) = \int_0^l F(x) dx$.

**Example: 1** Find the finite Fourier cosine transform of $F(x) = 1, 0 < x < \pi$.

**Solution:** By the definition of finite Fourier cosine transform of $F(x)$, we have

$$f_c(n) = \int_0^l F(x)\cos\frac{n\pi x}{l}dx$$

where $n$ is an integer.

Here $F(x) = 1$ and $l = \pi$ so we have

$$f_c(n) = \int_0^\pi 1.\cos nx\, dx = \left[\frac{\sin nx}{n}\right]_0^\pi$$

$$\Rightarrow f_c(n) = \left[\frac{\sin n\pi}{n} - 0\right]$$

$$\Rightarrow f_c(n) = 0$$

**Example: 2** Find the finite Fourier cosine transform of $F(x) = x, 0 < x < \pi$.

**Solution:** By the definition of finite Fourier cosine transform of $F(x)$, we have

$$f_c(n) = \int_0^l F(x)\cos\frac{n\pi x}{l}dx$$

where $n$ is an integer.

Here $F(x) = x$ and $l = \pi$ so we have

$$f_c(n) = \int_0^\pi x\cos nx\, dx = \left[x\frac{\sin nx}{n}\right]_0^\pi - \left[-\frac{\cos nx}{n^2}\right]_0^\pi$$

$$\Rightarrow f_c(n) = \left[\pi\frac{\sin n\pi}{n} - 0\right] + \left[\frac{\cos n\pi}{n^2} - \frac{1}{n^2}\right]$$

$$\Rightarrow f_c(n) = \left(\frac{cosn\pi - 1}{n^2}\right)$$

**Example: 3** Find the finite Fourier cosine transform of $F(x) = x^2, 0 < x < \pi$.

**Solution:** By the definition of finite Fourier cosine transform of $F(x)$, we have

$$f_c(n) = \int_0^l F(x)\cos\frac{n\pi x}{l} dx$$

where $n$ is an integer.

Here $F(x) = x^2$ and $l = \pi$ so we have

$$f_c(n) = \int_0^\pi x^2 \cos nx\, dx = \left[x^2 \frac{sinnx}{n}\right]_0^\pi - \int_0^\pi 2x\left(\frac{sinnx}{n}\right) dx$$

$$\Rightarrow f_c(n) = \left[\pi^2 \frac{sinn\pi}{n} - 0\right] - \frac{2}{n}\int_0^\pi x\, sinnx\, dx$$

$$\Rightarrow f_c(n) = -\frac{2}{n}\left\{\left[-x\frac{cosnx}{n}\right]_0^\pi - \left[-\frac{sinnx}{n^2}\right]_0^\pi\right\}$$

$$\Rightarrow f_c(n) = -\frac{2}{n}\left\{\left[-\pi\frac{cosn\pi}{n} + 0\right] + \left[\frac{sinn\pi}{n^2} - 0\right]\right\}$$

$$\Rightarrow f_c(n) = \frac{2\pi(cosn\pi)}{n^2}$$

**Example: 4** Find the finite Fourier cosine transform of $F(x) = e^x, 0 < x < 1$.

59

**Solution:** By the definition of finite Fourier cosine transform of $F(x)$, we have

$$f_c(n) = \int_0^l F(x)\cos\frac{n\pi x}{l} dx$$

where $n$ is an integer.

Here $F(x) = e^x$ and $l = 1$ so we have

$$f_c(n) = \int_0^1 e^x \cos n\pi x \, dx = \left[\frac{e^x}{1+n^2\pi^2}(\cos n\pi x + n\pi \sin n\pi x)\right]_0^1$$

$$\Rightarrow f_c(n) = \left[\frac{e}{1+n^2\pi^2}(\cos n\pi + n\pi \sin n\pi) - \frac{1}{1+n^2\pi^2}(1+0)\right]$$

$$\Rightarrow f_c(n) = \frac{1}{1+n^2\pi^2}[e\cos n\pi - 1]$$

**Example: 5** Find the finite Fourier cosine transform of the following function

$$F(x) = \begin{cases} x, & 0 \le x < \pi/2 \\ \pi - x, & \pi/2 < x \le \pi \end{cases}$$

**Solution:** By the definition of finite Fourier cosine transform of $F(x)$, we have

$$f_c(n) = \int_0^l F(x)\cos\frac{n\pi x}{l} dx$$

where $n$ is an integer.

Here $F(x) = \begin{cases} x, & 0 \leq x < \pi/2 \\ \pi - x, & \pi/2 < x \leq \pi \end{cases}$ and $l = \pi$ so we have

$$f_c(n) = \int_0^\pi F(x) \cos nx\, dx$$

$$\Rightarrow f_c(n) = \int_0^{\pi/2} F(x) \cos nx\, dx + \int_{\pi/2}^\pi F(x) \cos nx\, dx$$

$$\Rightarrow f_c(n) = \int_0^{\pi/2} x \cos nx\, dx + \int_{\pi/2}^\pi (\pi - x) \cos nx\, dx$$

$$\Rightarrow f_c(n) = \left[x \frac{\sin nx}{n}\right]_0^{\pi/2} - \left[-\frac{\cos nx}{n^2}\right]_0^{\pi/2} + \left[-(\pi-x)\frac{\sin nx}{n}\right]_{\pi/2}^\pi - \left[\frac{\cos nx}{n^2}\right]_{\pi/2}^\pi$$

$$\Rightarrow f_c(n) = \begin{bmatrix} \left\{\frac{\pi}{2n}\sin\frac{n\pi}{2}\right\} + \frac{1}{n^2}\left\{\cos\frac{n\pi}{2} - 1\right\} \\ -\left\{0 - \frac{\pi}{2n}\sin\frac{n\pi}{2}\right\} - \frac{1}{n^2}\left\{\cos n\pi - \cos\frac{n\pi}{2}\right\} \end{bmatrix}$$

$$\Rightarrow f_c(n) = \begin{bmatrix} \left\{\frac{\pi}{2n}\sin\frac{n\pi}{2}\right\} + \frac{1}{n^2}\left\{\cos\frac{n\pi}{2} - 1\right\} + \left\{\frac{\pi}{2n}\sin\frac{n\pi}{2}\right\} \\ -\frac{1}{n^2}\left\{\cos n\pi - \cos\frac{n\pi}{2}\right\} \end{bmatrix}$$

$$\Rightarrow f_c(n) = \frac{\pi}{n}\sin\frac{n\pi}{2} + \frac{1}{n^2}\left\{2\cos\frac{n\pi}{2} - \cos n\pi - 1\right\}$$

**Example: 6** Find the finite Fourier cosine transform of the following function

$$F(x) = \begin{cases} 0, & 0 \leq x < \pi/2 \\ 1, & \pi/2 < x \leq \pi \end{cases}$$

**Solution:** By the definition of finite Fourier cosine transform of $F(x)$, we have

$$f_c(n) = \int_0^l F(x)\cos\frac{n\pi x}{l} dx$$

where $n$ is an integer.

Here $F(x) = \begin{cases} 0, & 0 \leq x < \pi/2 \\ 1, & \pi/2 < x \leq \pi \end{cases}$ and $l = \pi$ so we have

$$f_c(n) = \int_0^\pi F(x)\cos nx\, dx$$

$$\Rightarrow f_c(n) = \int_0^{\pi/2} F(x)\cos nx\, dx + \int_{\pi/2}^\pi F(x)\cos nx\, dx$$

$$\Rightarrow f_c(n) = \int_0^{\pi/2} 0.\cos nx\, dx + \int_{\pi/2}^\pi 1.\cos nx\, dx = \left[\frac{\sin nx}{n}\right]_{\pi/2}^\pi$$

$$\Rightarrow f_c(n) = \frac{1}{n}\left\{\sin n\pi - \sin\frac{n\pi}{2}\right\} = \frac{1}{n}\left\{0 - \sin\frac{n\pi}{2}\right\}$$

$$\Rightarrow f_c(n) = -\frac{1}{n}\sin\frac{n\pi}{2}$$

**Example: 7** Find the finite Fourier cosine transform of the following function

$$F(x) = \begin{cases} 1, & 0 \leq x < \pi/2 \\ -1, & \pi/2 < x \leq \pi \end{cases}$$

**Solution:** By the definition of finite Fourier cosine transform of $F(x)$, we have

$$f_c(n) = \int_0^l F(x)\cos\frac{n\pi x}{l} dx$$

where $n$ is an integer.

Here $F(x) = \begin{cases} 1, & 0 \leq x < \pi/2 \\ -1, & \pi/2 < x \leq \pi \end{cases}$ and $l = \pi$ so we have

$$f_c(n) = \int_0^\pi F(x)\cos nx\, dx$$

$$\Rightarrow f_c(n) = \int_0^{\pi/2} F(x)\cos nx\, dx + \int_{\pi/2}^\pi F(x)\cos nx\, dx$$

$$\Rightarrow f_c(n) = \int_0^{\pi/2} 1.\cos nx\, dx + \int_{\pi/2}^\pi (-1).\cos nx\, dx$$

$$\Rightarrow f_c(n) = \int_0^{\pi/2} \cos nx\, dx - \int_{\pi/2}^\pi \cos nx\, dx$$

$$\Rightarrow f_c(n) = \left[\frac{\sin nx}{n}\right]_0^{\pi/2} - \left[\frac{\sin nx}{n}\right]_{\pi/2}^\pi$$

$$\Rightarrow f_c(n) = \frac{1}{n}\left\{\sin\frac{n\pi}{2} - 0\right\} - \frac{1}{n}\left\{\sin n\pi - \sin\frac{n\pi}{2}\right\}$$

$$\Rightarrow f_c(n) = \frac{1}{n}\left\{\sin\frac{n\pi}{2}\right\} - \frac{1}{n}\left\{0 - \sin\frac{n\pi}{2}\right\}$$

$$\Rightarrow f_c(n) = \frac{2}{n}\sin\frac{n\pi}{2}$$

## Exercise

1. Find the finite Fourier cosine transform of the function

$$F(x) = 2x, 0 < x < 4$$

Ans: $f_c(n) = \begin{cases} \frac{32}{n^2\pi^2}(\cos n\pi - 1), & n > 0 \\ 16, & n = 0 \end{cases}$

2. Find the finite Fourier cosine transform of the function

$$F(x) = \left(1 - \frac{x}{\pi}\right), 0 < x < \pi$$

Ans: $f_c(n) = \frac{1}{n^2\pi}[1 - (-1)^n]$

3. Find the finite Fourier cosine transform of the function

$$F(x) = \left(\frac{x}{4\pi}\right), 0 < x < \pi$$

Ans: $f_c(n) = \frac{1}{4n^2\pi}[(-1)^n - 1]$

4. Find the finite Fourier cosine transform of the function

$$F(x) = \left(1 - \frac{x}{\pi}\right)^2, 0 < x < \pi$$

Ans: $f_c(n) = \begin{cases} \frac{2}{n^2\pi}, & n > 0 \\ \frac{\pi}{3}, & n = 0 \end{cases}$

5. Find the finite Fourier sine transform of the function

$$F(x) = x(\pi - x), 0 < x < \pi$$

Ans: $f_s(n) = -\frac{\pi}{n^2}[1 + (-1)^n]$

# Chapter-6

# APPLICATIONS OF FOURIER TRANSFORMS

**Introduction:** In this chapter, we shall determine the solution of partial differential equations with the help of Fourier transform, Fourier sine transform, Fourier cosine transform, finite Fourier sine transform and finite Fourier cosine transform.

**Remark: 1** If $u(x,t)$ is the dependent variable in the given problem and the range of variable $x$ is $-\infty < x < \infty$ then Fourier transform should be used in the problem.

**Remark: 2** If $u(x,t)$ is the dependent variable in the given problem and its value at $x = 0$ is known in the problem then Fourier sine transform should be used in the problem.

**Remark: 3** If $u(x,t)$ is the dependent variable in the given problem and its derivative, i.e. $\frac{\partial u}{\partial x}$, value at $x = 0$ is known in the problem then Fourier cosine transform should be used in the problem.

**Remark: 4** If $u(x,t)$ is the dependent variable in the given problem and its value at two different boundary points are known in the problem then finite Fourier sine transform should be used in the problem.

**Remark: 5** If $u(x,t)$ is the dependent variable in the given problem and its derivative, i.e. $\frac{\partial u}{\partial x}$, value at two different boundary points are known in the problem then finite Fourier cosine transform should be used in the problem.

**Example: 1** Using Fourier transform, solve the following equation

$$\frac{\partial u}{\partial t} = \frac{\partial^2 u}{\partial x^2}, -\infty < x < \infty, t > 0$$

with $u(x, 0) = f(x)$

**Solution:** The given equation is

$$\frac{\partial u}{\partial t} = \frac{\partial^2 u}{\partial x^2}, -\infty < x < \infty, t > 0$$

Taking Fourier transform of both sides of above equation, we have

$$\int_{-\infty}^{\infty} \frac{\partial u}{\partial t} e^{ipx} \, dx = \int_{-\infty}^{\infty} \frac{\partial^2 u}{\partial x^2} e^{ipx} \, dx$$

$$\Rightarrow \frac{d}{dt} \int_{-\infty}^{\infty} u e^{ipx} \, dx = \left[ e^{ipx} \frac{\partial u}{\partial x} \right]_{-\infty}^{\infty} - \int_{-\infty}^{\infty} (ip) \frac{\partial u}{\partial x} e^{ipx} \, dx$$

$$\Rightarrow \frac{d\tilde{u}}{dt} = [0 - 0] - (ip) \int_{-\infty}^{\infty} \frac{\partial u}{\partial x} e^{ipx} \, dx$$

{Since $\partial u/\partial x \to 0$ as $x \to \infty$}

$$\Rightarrow \frac{d\tilde{u}}{dt} = -(ip)\left\{[e^{ipx} u]_{-\infty}^{\infty} - \int_{-\infty}^{\infty} (ip)ue^{ipx}\, dx\right\}$$

$$\Rightarrow \frac{d\tilde{u}}{dt} = -(ip)\left\{[0-0] - (ip)\int_{-\infty}^{\infty} ue^{ipx}\, dx\right\}$$

$$\{Since\ u \to 0\ as\ x \to \infty\}$$

$$\Rightarrow \frac{d\tilde{u}}{dt} = (ip)^2 \int_{-\infty}^{\infty} ue^{ipx}\, dx = -p^2 \tilde{u}$$

$$\Rightarrow \frac{d\tilde{u}}{dt} + p^2 \tilde{u} = 0$$

The solution of above equation is given by

$$\tilde{u} = Ae^{-p^2 t},\ \text{where } A \text{ is the arbitrary constant.}$$

Given $u(x, 0) = f(x)$, so when $t = 0, \tilde{u} = \tilde{f}(p) = \int_{-\infty}^{\infty} f(x)e^{ipx}\, dx$

Using this result in above equation, we have

$$\tilde{f}(p) = A$$

Hence, we have

$$\tilde{u} = \tilde{f}(p)e^{-p^2 t}$$

Now, taking inverse Fourier transform of both sides of above equation, we have

$$u(x,t) = \frac{1}{2\pi} \int_{-\infty}^{\infty} \tilde{u} e^{-ipx} \, dp$$

$$\Rightarrow u(x,t) = \frac{1}{2\pi} \int_{-\infty}^{\infty} \tilde{f}(p) e^{-p^2 t} e^{-ipx} \, dp$$

**Example: 2** Using Fourier transform, solve the following initial boundary value problem:

$$\frac{\partial u}{\partial t} = c^2 \frac{\partial^2 u}{\partial x^2}, \quad -\infty < x < \infty, t > 0$$

$$\text{with } u(x,0) = \begin{cases} 1, & -1 < x < 0 \\ -1, & 0 < x < 1 \\ 0, & otherwise \end{cases}$$

**Solution:** The given equation is

$$\frac{\partial u}{\partial t} = c^2 \frac{\partial^2 u}{\partial x^2}, \quad -\infty < x < \infty, t > 0$$

Taking Fourier transform of both sides of above equation, we have

$$\int_{-\infty}^{\infty} \frac{\partial u}{\partial t} e^{ipx} \, dx = c^2 \int_{-\infty}^{\infty} \frac{\partial^2 u}{\partial x^2} e^{ipx} \, dx$$

$$\Rightarrow \frac{d}{dt} \int_{-\infty}^{\infty} u e^{ipx} \, dx = c^2 \left\{ \left[ e^{ipx} \frac{\partial u}{\partial x} \right]_{-\infty}^{\infty} - \int_{-\infty}^{\infty} (ip) \frac{\partial u}{\partial x} e^{ipx} \, dx \right\}$$

$$\Rightarrow \frac{d\tilde{u}}{dt} = c^2 \left\{ [0-0] - (ip) \int_{-\infty}^{\infty} \frac{\partial u}{\partial x} e^{ipx} \, dx \right\}$$

$$\{Since\ \partial u/\partial x \to 0\ as\ x \to \infty\}$$

$$\Rightarrow \frac{d\tilde{u}}{dt} = -(ip)c^2 \left\{ [e^{ipx} u]_{-\infty}^{\infty} - \int_{-\infty}^{\infty} (ip)ue^{ipx}\ dx \right\}$$

$$\Rightarrow \frac{d\tilde{u}}{dt} = -(ip)c^2 \left\{ [0-0] - (ip)\int_{-\infty}^{\infty} ue^{ipx}\ dx \right\}$$

$$\{Since\ u \to 0\ as\ x \to \infty\}$$

$$\Rightarrow \frac{d\tilde{u}}{dt} = (ipc)^2 \int_{-\infty}^{\infty} ue^{ipx}\ dx = -p^2 c^2 \tilde{u}$$

$$\Rightarrow \frac{d\tilde{u}}{dt} + p^2 c^2 \tilde{u} = 0$$

The solution of above equation is given by

$$\tilde{u} = A e^{-p^2 c^2 t},\ \text{where } A \text{ is the arbitrary constant.}$$

Given $u(x,0) = \begin{cases} 1, & -1 < x < 0 \\ -1, & 0 < x < 1 \\ 0, & otherwise \end{cases}$, so when $t = 0$,

$$\tilde{u} = \int_{-\infty}^{\infty} ue^{ipx}\ dx$$

$$\Rightarrow \tilde{u} = \int_{-\infty}^{-1} ue^{ipx}\ dx + \int_{-1}^{0} ue^{ipx}\ dx + \int_{0}^{1} ue^{ipx}\ dx + \int_{1}^{\infty} ue^{ipx}\ dx$$

$$\Rightarrow \tilde{u} = \int_{-\infty}^{-1} 0.e^{ipx}\, dx + \int_{-1}^{0} 1.e^{ipx}\, dx + \int_{0}^{1} (-1).e^{ipx}\, dx + \int_{1}^{\infty} 0.e^{ipx}\, dx$$

$$\Rightarrow \tilde{u} = \int_{-1}^{0} e^{ipx}\, dx - \int_{0}^{1} e^{ipx}\, dx$$

$$\Rightarrow \tilde{u} = \left[\frac{e^{ipx}}{ip}\right]_{-1}^{0} - \left[\frac{e^{ipx}}{ip}\right]_{0}^{1}$$

$$\Rightarrow \tilde{u} = \left[\frac{1}{ip} - \frac{e^{-ip}}{ip}\right] - \left[\frac{e^{ip}}{ip} - \frac{1}{ip}\right]$$

$$\Rightarrow \tilde{u} = \left[\frac{2}{ip} - \frac{(e^{ip} + e^{-ip})}{ip}\right] = \left[\frac{2}{ip} - \frac{2\cos p}{ip}\right]$$

$$\Rightarrow \tilde{u} = \frac{2}{ip}(1 - \cos p)$$

Using this condition in the equation $\tilde{u} = Ae^{-p^2 c^2 t}$, we have

$$A = \frac{2}{ip}(1 - \cos p)$$

Hence, we have

$$\tilde{u} = \frac{2}{ip}(1 - \cos p)e^{-p^2 c^2 t}$$

Taking inverse Fourier transform of both sides of above equation, we have

$$u(x,t) = \frac{1}{2\pi}\int_{-\infty}^{\infty} \tilde{u} e^{-ipx} \, dp$$

$$\Rightarrow u(x,t) = \frac{1}{2\pi}\int_{-\infty}^{\infty} \frac{2}{ip}(1-\cos p) e^{-p^2 c^2 t} e^{-ipx} \, dp$$

$$\Rightarrow u(x,t) = \frac{1}{i\pi}\int_{-\infty}^{\infty} \frac{(1-\cos p)}{p} e^{-p^2 c^2 t} e^{-ipx} \, dp$$

**Example: 3** An infinite string is initially at rest and that the initial displacement is $f(x), -\infty < x < \infty$. Determine the displacement $y(x,t)$ of the string.

**Solution:** The equation for the vibration of the string is governed by

$$\frac{\partial^2 y}{\partial t^2} = c^2 \frac{\partial^2 y}{\partial x^2}, \quad -\infty < x < \infty, t > 0$$

Taking Fourier transform of both sides of above equation, we have

$$\int_{-\infty}^{\infty} \frac{\partial^2 y}{\partial t^2} e^{ipx} \, dx = c^2 \int_{-\infty}^{\infty} \frac{\partial^2 y}{\partial x^2} e^{ipx} \, dx$$

$$\Rightarrow \frac{d^2}{dt^2}\int_{-\infty}^{\infty} y e^{ipx} \, dx = c^2 \left\{ \left[ e^{ipx}\frac{\partial y}{\partial x}\right]_{-\infty}^{\infty} - \int_{-\infty}^{\infty} (ip)\frac{\partial y}{\partial x} e^{ipx} \, dx \right\}$$

$$\Rightarrow \frac{d^2 \tilde{y}}{dt^2} = c^2 \left\{ [0-0] - (ip)\int_{-\infty}^{\infty} \frac{\partial y}{\partial x} e^{ipx} \, dx \right\}$$

{Since $\partial y/\partial x \to 0$ as $x \to \infty$}

$$\Rightarrow \frac{d^2\tilde{y}}{dt^2} = -(ip)c^2 \left\{ \left[e^{ipx} y\right]_{-\infty}^{\infty} - \int_{-\infty}^{\infty} (ip) y e^{ipx}\, dx \right\}$$

$$\Rightarrow \frac{d^2\tilde{y}}{dt^2} = -(ip)c^2 \left\{ [0-0] - (ip) \int_{-\infty}^{\infty} y e^{ipx}\, dx \right\}$$

$$\{\text{Since } y \to 0 \text{ as } x \to \infty\}$$

$$\Rightarrow \frac{d^2\tilde{y}}{dt^2} = (ipc)^2 \int_{-\infty}^{\infty} y e^{ipx}\, dx = -p^2 c^2 \tilde{y}$$

$$\Rightarrow \frac{d^2\tilde{y}}{dt^2} + p^2 c^2 \tilde{y} = 0$$

The solution of above equation is given by

$$\tilde{y} = A\cos pct + B\sin pct, \text{ where } A, B \text{ are the arbitrary constants}$$

$$\left\{ \text{Since } \begin{array}{c} A.E.\ m^2 + p^2c^2 = 0 \Rightarrow m = pci \\ C.F. = A\cos pct + B\sin pct \\ P.I. = 0 \\ \tilde{y} = C.F. + P.I. = A\cos pct + B\sin pct \end{array} \right\}$$

Now $\frac{\partial \tilde{y}}{\partial t} = -pcA\sin pct + Bpc\cos pct$

Since string is initially at rest so $\frac{\partial y}{\partial t} = 0$ at $t = 0$

$\Rightarrow$ at $t = 0, \frac{\partial \tilde{y}}{\partial t} = 0$

Using this in $\frac{\partial \tilde{y}}{\partial t} = -pcAsinpct + Bpccospct$, we have

$$B = 0$$

Putting $B = 0$ in the equation $\tilde{y} = Acospct + Bsinpct$, we have

$$\tilde{y} = Acospct$$

Since initial displacement is $f(x), -\infty < x < \infty$ so at $t = 0, y = f(x)$

$\Rightarrow$ at $t = 0, \tilde{y} = \int_{-\infty}^{\infty} f(x)e^{ipx} dx = \tilde{f}(p)$

Using this condition in above equation, we have

$$A = \tilde{f}(p)$$

Thus,

$$\tilde{y} = \tilde{f}(p)cospct$$

Taking inverse Fourier transform of both sides of above equation, we have

$$y(x,t) = \frac{1}{2\pi}\int_{-\infty}^{\infty} \tilde{y}e^{-ipx} dp$$

$$\Rightarrow y(x,t) = \frac{1}{2\pi}\int_{-\infty}^{\infty} e^{-ipx} \tilde{f}(p)cospct\, dp$$

$$\Rightarrow y(x,t) = \frac{1}{2\pi}\int_{-\infty}^{\infty} e^{-ipx} \tilde{f}(p)\left[\frac{e^{ipct} + e^{-ipct}}{2}\right] dp$$

$$\Rightarrow y(x,t) = \frac{1}{2}\left\{\frac{1}{2\pi}\int_{-\infty}^{\infty} e^{-ip(x-ct)} \tilde{f}(p)\, dp + \frac{1}{2\pi}\int_{-\infty}^{\infty} e^{-ip(x+ct)} \tilde{f}(p)\, dp\right\}$$

$$\Rightarrow y(x,t) = \frac{1}{2}\{f(x-ct) + f(x-ct)\}$$

**Example: 4** Solve the following differential equation

$$\frac{\partial u}{\partial t} = k\frac{\partial^2 u}{\partial x^2}, x \geq 0, t \geq 0$$

under the following three conditions

- $u(0,t) = u_0, \; t > 0$
- $u(x,0) = 0, \; x \geq 0$
- $u(x,t)$ is bounded.

**Solution:** The given equation is

$$\frac{\partial u}{\partial t} = k\frac{\partial^2 u}{\partial x^2}, x \geq 0, t \geq 0$$

Taking Fourier sine transform of both sides of above equation, we have

$$\int_0^\infty \frac{\partial u}{\partial t} \sin px\, dx = k \int_0^\infty \frac{\partial^2 u}{\partial x^2} \sin px\, dx$$

$$\Rightarrow \frac{d}{dt}\int_0^\infty u \sin px\, dx = k\left\{\left[\sin px \frac{\partial u}{\partial x}\right]_0^\infty - p\int_0^\infty \cos px \frac{\partial u}{\partial x} dx\right\}$$

$$\Rightarrow \frac{d\widetilde{u_s}}{dt} = k\left\{[0-0] - p\int_0^\infty \cos px \frac{\partial u}{\partial x} dx\right\}$$

{Since $\partial u/\partial x \to 0$ as $x \to \infty$}

$$\Rightarrow \frac{d\widetilde{u_s}}{dt} = -kp\left\{[u\cos px]_0^\infty + p\int_0^\infty u\sin px\, dx\right\}$$

$$\Rightarrow \frac{d\widetilde{u_s}}{dt} = -kp\left\{[0-u_0] + p\int_0^\infty u\sin px\, dx\right\}$$

{Since $u \to 0$ as $x \to \infty$, and $u(0,t) = u_0, t > 0$}

$$\Rightarrow \frac{d\widetilde{u_s}}{dt} = -kp^2\widetilde{u_s} + kpu_0$$

$$\Rightarrow \frac{d\widetilde{u_s}}{dt} + kp^2\widetilde{u_s} = kpu_0$$

The solution of above equation is given by

$$\widetilde{u_s} = Ae^{-p^2 kt} + \frac{u_0}{p}$$

$$\left\{\text{Since } \begin{array}{c} A.E.\ m + kp^2 = 0 \Rightarrow m = -kp^2 \\ C.F. = Ae^{-p^2 kt} \\ P.I. = \frac{1}{D+kp^2} kpu_0 = \frac{kpu_0}{kp^2} = \frac{u_0}{p} \\ \widetilde{u_s} = C.F. + P.I. \end{array}\right\}$$

Given $u(x, 0) = 0$, $x \geq 0$ so when $t = 0, \widetilde{u_s} = 0$

Using this condition in the equation $\widetilde{u_s} = Ae^{-p^2 kt} + \frac{u_0}{p}$, we have

$$0 = A + \frac{u_0}{p} \Rightarrow A = -\frac{u_0}{p}$$

Hence, we have

$$\widetilde{u_s} = -\frac{u_0}{p}e^{-p^2 kt} + \frac{u_0}{p}$$

$$\Rightarrow \widetilde{u_s} = \frac{u_0}{p}\left(1 - e^{-p^2 kt}\right)$$

Taking inverse Fourier sine transform of both sides of above equation, we have

$$u(x,t) = \frac{2}{\pi}\int_0^\infty \widetilde{u_s} \sin px \, dp$$

$$\Rightarrow u(x,t) = \frac{2}{\pi}\int_0^\infty \frac{u_0}{p}\left(1 - e^{-p^2 kt}\right) \sin px \, dp$$

**Example: 5** Solve the equation

$$\frac{\partial u}{\partial t} = \frac{\partial^2 u}{\partial x^2}, x > 0, t > 0$$

subject to the following three conditions

(i)    $u = 0$ when $x = 0, t > 0$

(ii)    $u = \begin{cases} 1, & 0 < x < 1 \\ 0, & x \geq 1 \end{cases}$ when $t = 0$

(iii) $u(x, t)$ is bounded.

**Solution:** The given equation is

$$\frac{\partial u}{\partial t} = \frac{\partial^2 u}{\partial x^2}, x > 0, t > 0$$

Taking Fourier sine transform of both sides of above equation, we have

$$\int_0^\infty \frac{\partial u}{\partial t} \sin px\, dx = \int_0^\infty \frac{\partial^2 u}{\partial x^2} \sin px\, dx$$

$$\Rightarrow \frac{d}{dt} \int_0^\infty u \sin px\, dx = \left\{ \left[\sin px \frac{\partial u}{\partial x}\right]_0^\infty - p \int_0^\infty \cos px \frac{\partial u}{\partial x} dx \right\}$$

$$\Rightarrow \frac{d\widetilde{u}_s}{dt} = \left\{ [0 - 0] - p \int_0^\infty \cos px \frac{\partial u}{\partial x} dx \right\}$$

{Since $\partial u/\partial x \to 0$ as $x \to \infty$}

$$\Rightarrow \frac{d\widetilde{u}_s}{dt} = -p\left\{ [u\cos px]_0^\infty + p \int_0^\infty u \sin px\, dx \right\}$$

$$\Rightarrow \frac{d\widetilde{u}_s}{dt} = -p\left\{ [0 - 0] + p \int_0^\infty u \sin px\, dx \right\}$$

{Since $u \to 0$ as $x \to \infty$, and $u(0,t) = 0, t > 0$}

$$\Rightarrow \frac{d\widetilde{u}_s}{dt} = -p^2 \widetilde{u}_s$$

$$\Rightarrow \frac{d\widetilde{u_s}}{dt} + p^2 \widetilde{u_s} = 0$$

The solution of above equation is given by

$$\widetilde{u_s} = Ae^{-p^2 t}$$

Given $u = \begin{cases} 1, & 0 < x < 1 \\ 0, & x \geq 1 \end{cases}$ when $t = 0$, so when $t = 0$,

$$\widetilde{u_s} = \int_0^\infty u \sin px \, dx$$

$$\Rightarrow \widetilde{u_s} = \int_0^1 u \sin px \, dx + \int_1^\infty u \sin px \, dx$$

$$\Rightarrow \widetilde{u_s} = \int_0^1 1 \cdot \sin px \, dx + \int_1^\infty 0 \cdot \sin px \, dx$$

$$\Rightarrow \widetilde{u_s} = \int_0^1 \sin px \, dx = \left[ -\frac{\cos px}{p} \right]_0^1$$

$$\Rightarrow \widetilde{u_s} = \frac{(1 - \cos p)}{p}$$

Using this result in the equation $\widetilde{u_s} = Ae^{-p^2 t}$, we have

$$A = \frac{(1 - \cos p)}{p}$$

Hence, we have

78

$$\widetilde{u_s} = \frac{(1-cosp)}{p} e^{-p^2 t}$$

Taking inverse Fourier sine transform of both sides of above equation, we have

$$u(x,t) = \frac{2}{\pi} \int_0^\infty \widetilde{u_s} \sin px \, dp$$

$$\Rightarrow u(x,t) = \frac{2}{\pi} \int_0^\infty \frac{(1-cosp)}{p} e^{-p^2 t} \sin px \, dp$$

**Example: 6** Apply appropriate Fourier transform to solve the partial differential equation

$$\frac{\partial u}{\partial t} = \frac{\partial^2 u}{\partial x^2}, x > 0, t > 0$$

subject to the following three conditions

(i) $u_x(0,t) = 0$

(ii) $u(x,0) = \begin{cases} x, & 0 \leq x \leq 1 \\ 0, & x > 1 \end{cases}$

(iii) $u(x,t)$ is bounded.

**Solution:** The given equation is

$$\frac{\partial u}{\partial t} = \frac{\partial^2 u}{\partial x^2}, x > 0, t > 0$$

Taking Fourier cosine transform of both sides of above equation, we have

$$\int_0^\infty \frac{\partial u}{\partial t} \cos px\, dx = \int_0^\infty \frac{\partial^2 u}{\partial x^2} \cos px\, dx$$

$$\Rightarrow \frac{d}{dt}\int_0^\infty u\cos px\, dx = \left\{\left[\cos px \frac{\partial u}{\partial x}\right]_0^\infty + p\int_0^\infty \sin px \frac{\partial u}{\partial x} dx\right\}$$

$$\Rightarrow \frac{d\widetilde{u_c}}{dt} = \left\{[0-0] + p\int_0^\infty \sin px \frac{\partial u}{\partial x} dx\right\}$$

$$\left\{\text{Since } \frac{\partial u}{\partial x} \to 0 \text{ as } x \to \infty \text{ and } u_x(0,t) = 0\right\}$$

$$\Rightarrow \frac{d\widetilde{u_c}}{dt} = p\left\{[u\sin px]_0^\infty - p\int_0^\infty u\cos px\, dx\right\}$$

$$\Rightarrow \frac{d\widetilde{u_c}}{dt} = p\left\{[0-0] - p\int_0^\infty u\cos px\, dx\right\}$$

$$\{\text{Since } u \to 0 \text{ as } x \to \infty\}$$

$$\Rightarrow \frac{d\widetilde{u_c}}{dt} = -p^2 \widetilde{u_c}$$

$$\Rightarrow \frac{d\widetilde{u_c}}{dt} + p^2 \widetilde{u_c} = 0$$

The solution of above equation is given by

$$\widetilde{u_c} = Ae^{-p^2 t}$$

Given $u(x, 0) = \begin{cases} x, & 0 \leq x \leq 1 \\ 0, & x > 1 \end{cases}$, so when $t = 0$,

$$\widetilde{u}_c = \int_0^\infty u \cos px \, dx$$

$$\Rightarrow \widetilde{u}_c = \int_0^1 u \cos px \, dx + \int_1^\infty u \cos px \, dx$$

$$\Rightarrow \widetilde{u}_c = \int_0^1 x \cos px \, dx + \int_1^\infty 0 \cdot \cos px \, dx$$

$$\Rightarrow \widetilde{u}_c = \int_0^1 x \cos px \, dx = \left[x \frac{\sin px}{p}\right]_0^1 - \left[-\frac{\cos px}{p^2}\right]_0^1$$

$$\Rightarrow \widetilde{u}_c = \frac{\sin p}{p} + \frac{(\cos p - 1)}{p^2}$$

$$\Rightarrow \widetilde{u}_c = \left(\frac{p \sin p + \cos p - 1}{p^2}\right)$$

Using this result in the equation $\widetilde{u}_c = A e^{-p^2 t}$, we have

$$A = \left(\frac{p \sin p + \cos p - 1}{p^2}\right)$$

Hence, we have

$$\widetilde{u}_c = \left(\frac{p \sin p + \cos p - 1}{p^2}\right) e^{-p^2 t}$$

Taking inverse Fourier cosine transform of both sides of above equation, we have

$$u(x,t) = \frac{2}{\pi} \int_0^\infty \widetilde{u_c} \sin px \, dp$$

$$\Rightarrow u(x,t) = \frac{2}{\pi} \int_0^\infty \left( \frac{p \sin p + \cos p - 1}{p^2} \right) e^{-p^2 t} \sin px \, dp$$

**Example: 7** Use finite Fourier transform to solve the partial differential equation

$$\frac{\partial u}{\partial t} = \frac{\partial^2 u}{\partial x^2}, 0 < x < 4, t > 0$$

subject to the following three conditions

(i) $u(0,t) = 0, \ t > 0$

(ii) $u(4,t) = 0, \ t > 0$

(iii) $u(x,0) = 2x$, where $0 < x < 4$.

**Solution:** The given equation is

$$\frac{\partial u}{\partial t} = \frac{\partial^2 u}{\partial x^2}, 0 < x < 4, t > 0$$

Taking finite Fourier sine transform of both sides of above equation, we have

$$\int_0^4 \frac{\partial u}{\partial t} \sin \frac{p\pi x}{4} \, dx = \int_0^4 \frac{\partial^2 u}{\partial x^2} \sin \frac{p\pi x}{4} \, dx$$

$$\Rightarrow \frac{d}{dt}\int_0^4 u\sin\left(\frac{p\pi x}{4}\right)dx = \left\{\begin{array}{l}\left[\frac{\partial u}{\partial x}\sin\left(\frac{p\pi x}{4}\right)\right]_0^4 \\ -\int_0^4 \left(\frac{p\pi}{4}\right)\cos\left(\frac{p\pi x}{4}\right)\frac{\partial u}{\partial x}dx\end{array}\right\}$$

$$\Rightarrow \frac{d\widetilde{u_s}}{dt} = -\left(\frac{p\pi}{4}\right)\int_0^4 \cos\left(\frac{p\pi x}{4}\right)\frac{\partial u}{\partial x}dx$$

$$\Rightarrow \frac{d\widetilde{u_s}}{dt} = -\left(\frac{p\pi}{4}\right)\left\{\left[u\cos\left(\frac{p\pi x}{4}\right)\right]_0^4 + \left(\frac{p\pi}{4}\right)\int_0^4 u\sin\left(\frac{p\pi x}{4}\right)dx\right\}$$

$$\Rightarrow \frac{d\widetilde{u_s}}{dt} = -\left(\frac{p\pi}{4}\right)\left\{[u(4,t)\cos(p\pi) - u(0,t)] + \left(\frac{p\pi}{4}\right)\int_0^4 u\sin\left(\frac{p\pi x}{4}\right)dx\right\}$$

$$\Rightarrow \frac{d\widetilde{u_s}}{dt} = -\left(\frac{p\pi}{4}\right)\left\{[0-0] + \left(\frac{p\pi}{4}\right)\int_0^4 u\sin\left(\frac{p\pi x}{4}\right)dx\right\}$$

{Since $u(0,t) = 0, u(4,t) = 0, t > 0$}

$$\Rightarrow \frac{d\widetilde{u_s}}{dt} = -\left(\frac{p\pi}{4}\right)^2 \int_0^4 u\sin\left(\frac{p\pi x}{4}\right)dx$$

$$\Rightarrow \frac{d\widetilde{u_s}}{dt} + \left(\frac{p^2\pi^2}{16}\right)\widetilde{u_s} = 0$$

The solution of above equation is given by

$$\widetilde{u_s} = Ae^{-\left(\frac{p^2\pi^2}{16}\right)t}$$

Given $u(x,0) = 2x$, where $0 < x < 4$, so when $t = 0$,

$$\widetilde{u}_s = \int_0^4 u \sin\left(\frac{p\pi x}{4}\right) dx$$

$$\Rightarrow \widetilde{u}_s = \int_0^4 2x \sin\left(\frac{p\pi x}{4}\right) dx$$

$$\Rightarrow \widetilde{u}_s = 2\left\{\left[-x\frac{\cos\left(\frac{p\pi x}{4}\right)}{\left(\frac{p\pi}{4}\right)}\right]_0^4 + \left[\frac{\sin\left(\frac{p\pi x}{4}\right)}{\left(\frac{p^2\pi^2}{16}\right)}\right]_0^4\right\}$$

$$\Rightarrow \widetilde{u}_s = -\frac{8}{p\pi}[4\cos p\pi]$$

$$\Rightarrow \widetilde{u}_s = -\frac{32}{p\pi}\cos p\pi$$

$$\Rightarrow \widetilde{u}_s = \frac{32}{p\pi}(-1)^{p+1}$$

Using this result in the equation $\widetilde{u}_s = Ae^{-\left(\frac{p^2\pi^2}{16}\right)t}$, we have

$$A = \frac{32}{p\pi}(-1)^{p+1}$$

Hence, we have

$$\widetilde{u}_s = \frac{32}{p\pi}(-1)^{p+1} e^{-\left(\frac{p^2\pi^2}{16}\right)t}$$

Taking inverse finite Fourier sine transform of both sides of above equation, we have

$$u(x,t) = \frac{2}{4}\sum_{p=1}^{\infty} \widetilde{u_s} \sin\left(\frac{p\pi x}{4}\right)$$

$$\Rightarrow u(x,t) = \frac{1}{2}\sum_{p=1}^{\infty} \frac{32}{p\pi}(-1)^{p+1} e^{-\left(\frac{p^2\pi^2}{16}\right)t} \sin\left(\frac{p\pi x}{4}\right)$$

$$\Rightarrow u(x,t) = \frac{16}{\pi}\sum_{p=1}^{\infty} \frac{1}{p}(-1)^{p+1} e^{-\left(\frac{p^2\pi^2}{16}\right)t} \sin\left(\frac{p\pi x}{4}\right)$$

**Example: 8** Use finite Fourier transform to solve the partial differential equation

$$\frac{\partial u}{\partial t} = \frac{\partial^2 u}{\partial x^2}, 0 < x < \pi, t > 0$$

subject to the following three conditions

(i) $u(0,t) = 0, \ t > 0$

(ii) $u(\pi,t) = 0, \ t > 0$

(iii) $u(x,0) = 2x$, where $0 < x < \pi$.

**Solution:** The given equation is

$$\frac{\partial u}{\partial t} = \frac{\partial^2 u}{\partial x^2}, 0 < x < \pi, t > 0$$

Taking finite Fourier sine transform of both sides of above equation, we have

$$\int_0^\pi \frac{\partial u}{\partial t} \sin px\, dx = \int_0^\pi \frac{\partial^2 u}{\partial x^2} \sin px\, dx$$

$$\Rightarrow \frac{d}{dt}\int_0^\pi u \sin px\, dx = \left\{ \begin{array}{l} \left[\frac{\partial u}{\partial x}\sin px\right]_0^\pi \\ -\int_0^\pi p\cos px\, \frac{\partial u}{\partial x}dx \end{array} \right\}$$

$$\Rightarrow \frac{d\widetilde{u_s}}{dt} = -p\int_0^\pi \cos px\, \frac{\partial u}{\partial x}dx$$

$$\Rightarrow \frac{d\widetilde{u_s}}{dt} = -p\left\{[u\cos px]_0^\pi + p\int_0^\pi u\sin px\, dx\right\}$$

$$\Rightarrow \frac{d\widetilde{u_s}}{dt} = -p\left\{[u(\pi,t)\cos(p\pi) - u(0,t)] + p\int_0^\pi u\sin px\, dx\right\}$$

$$\Rightarrow \frac{d\widetilde{u_s}}{dt} = -p\left\{[0-0] + p\int_0^\pi u\sin px\, dx\right\}$$

$$\{Since\ u(0,t) = 0, u(\pi,t) = 0, t > 0\ \}$$

$$\Rightarrow \frac{d\widetilde{u_s}}{dt} = -p^2 \int_0^\pi u\sin px\, dx$$

$$\Rightarrow \frac{d\widetilde{u_s}}{dt} + p^2 \widetilde{u_s} = 0$$

The solution of above equation is given by

$$\widetilde{u_s} = Ae^{-p^2 t}$$

Given $u(x, 0) = 2x$, where $0 < x < \pi$, so when $t = 0$,

$$\widetilde{u_s} = \int_0^\pi u \sin px \, dx$$

$$\Rightarrow \widetilde{u_s} = \int_0^\pi 2x \sin px \, dx$$

$$\Rightarrow \widetilde{u_s} = 2\left\{\left[-x\frac{\cos px}{p}\right]_0^\pi + \left[\frac{\sin px}{p^2}\right]_0^\pi\right\}$$

$$\Rightarrow \widetilde{u_s} = -\frac{2}{p}[\pi \cos p\pi]$$

$$\Rightarrow \widetilde{u_s} = -\frac{2\pi}{p}\cos p\pi$$

$$\Rightarrow \widetilde{u_s} = \frac{2\pi}{p}(-1)^{p+1}$$

Using this result in the equation $\widetilde{u_s} = Ae^{-p^2 t}$, we have

$$A = \frac{2\pi}{p}(-1)^{p+1}$$

Hence, we have

$$\widetilde{u_s} = \frac{2\pi}{p}(-1)^{p+1} e^{-p^2 t}$$

Taking inverse finite Fourier sine transform of both sides of above equation, we have

$$u(x,t) = \frac{2}{\pi}\sum_{p=1}^{\infty} \widetilde{u_s} \sin px$$

$$\Rightarrow u(x,t) = \frac{2}{\pi}\sum_{p=1}^{\infty} \frac{2\pi}{p}(-1)^{p+1} e^{-p^2 t} \sin px$$

$$\Rightarrow u(x,t) = 4\sum_{p=1}^{\infty} \frac{1}{p}(-1)^{p+1} e^{-p^2 t} \sin px$$

**Example: 9** Use finite Fourier cosine transform to solve the partial differential equation

$$\frac{\partial u}{\partial t} = k\frac{\partial^2 u}{\partial x^2}, 0 < x < \pi, t > 0$$

with the following boundary and initial conditions

(i) $\frac{\partial u}{\partial x} = 0$, when $x = 0$, $t > 0$

(ii) $\frac{\partial u}{\partial x} = 0$, when $x = \pi$, $t > 0$

(iii) $u(x,0) = f(x)$, where $0 < x < \pi$.

**Solution:** The given equation is

$$\frac{\partial u}{\partial t} = k \frac{\partial^2 u}{\partial x^2}, 0 < x < \pi, t > 0$$

Taking finite Fourier cosine transform of both sides of above equation, we have

$$\int_0^\pi \frac{\partial u}{\partial t} \cos px\, dx = k \int_0^\pi \frac{\partial^2 u}{\partial x^2} \cos px\, dx$$

$$\Rightarrow \frac{d}{dt} \int_0^\pi u \cos px\, dx = k \left\{ \left[\frac{\partial u}{\partial x} \cos px\right]_0^\pi + \int_0^\pi p \sin px \frac{\partial u}{\partial x} dx \right\}$$

$$\Rightarrow \frac{d\widetilde{u_c}}{dt} = k \left\{ \left[\left(\frac{\partial u}{\partial x}\right)_{x=\pi} \cos p\pi - \left(\frac{\partial u}{\partial x}\right)_{x=0}\right] + p \int_0^\pi \sin px \frac{\partial u}{\partial x} dx \right\}$$

$$\Rightarrow \frac{d\widetilde{u_c}}{dt} = k \left\{ [0 - 0] + p \int_0^\pi \sin px \frac{\partial u}{\partial x} dx \right\}$$

$$\left\{ \text{Since } \frac{\partial u}{\partial x} = 0, \text{when } x = 0, \quad \frac{\partial u}{\partial x} = 0, \text{when } x = \pi, \quad t > 0 \right\}$$

$$\Rightarrow \frac{d\widetilde{u_c}}{dt} = pk \int_0^\pi \sin px \frac{\partial u}{\partial x} dx$$

$$\Rightarrow \frac{d\widetilde{u_c}}{dt} = pk \left\{ [u \sin px]_0^\pi - p \int_0^\pi u \cos px\, dx \right\}$$

$$\Rightarrow \frac{d\widetilde{u_c}}{dt} = -p^2 k \int_0^\pi u \cos px\, dx$$

$$\Rightarrow \frac{d\widetilde{u_c}}{dt} + p^2 k \widetilde{u_c} = 0$$

The solution of above equation is given by

$$\widetilde{u_c} = Ae^{-p^2 kt}$$

Given $u(x, 0) = f(x)$, where $0 < x < \pi$, so when $t = 0$,

$$\widetilde{u_c} = \int_0^\pi f(x) \cos px\, dx = \widetilde{f_c}(p)$$

Using this result in the equation $\widetilde{u_c} = Ae^{-p^2 kt}$, we have

$$A = \widetilde{f_c}(p)$$

Hence, we have

$$\widetilde{u_c} = \widetilde{f_c}(p) e^{-p^2 kt}$$

Taking inverse finite Fourier cosine transform of both sides of above equation, we have

$$u(x, t) = \frac{2}{\pi} \sum_{p=1}^{\infty} \widetilde{u_c} \cos px$$

$$\Rightarrow u(x, t) = \frac{2}{\pi} \sum_{p=1}^{\infty} \widetilde{f_c}(p) e^{-p^2 kt} \cos px$$

where

$$\tilde{f_c}(p) = \int_0^\pi f(x)\cos px\, dx.$$

**Example: 10** Use finite Fourier sine transform to solve the partial differential equation

$$\frac{\partial u}{\partial t} = \frac{\partial^2 u}{\partial x^2}, 0 < x < 6, t > 0$$

subject to the following three conditions

(i) $u(0,t) = 0, \ t > 0$

(ii) $u(6,t) = 0, \ t > 0$

(iii) $u(x,0) = \begin{cases} 1, & 0 < x < 3 \\ 0, & 3 < x < 6 \end{cases}.$

**Solution:** The given equation is

$$\frac{\partial u}{\partial t} = \frac{\partial^2 u}{\partial x^2}, 0 < x < 6, t > 0$$

Taking finite Fourier sine transform of both sides of above equation, we have

$$\int_0^6 \frac{\partial u}{\partial t} \sin\left(\frac{p\pi x}{6}\right) dx = \int_0^6 \frac{\partial^2 u}{\partial x^2} \sin\left(\frac{p\pi x}{6}\right) dx$$

$$\Rightarrow \frac{d}{dt}\int_0^6 u\sin\left(\frac{p\pi x}{6}\right)dx = \left\{\begin{array}{l}\left[\frac{\partial u}{\partial x}\sin\left(\frac{p\pi x}{6}\right)\right]_0^6 \\ -\int_0^6 \left(\frac{p\pi}{6}\right)\cos\left(\frac{p\pi x}{6}\right)\frac{\partial u}{\partial x}dx\end{array}\right\}$$

$$\Rightarrow \frac{d\widetilde{u}_s}{dt} = -\left(\frac{p\pi}{6}\right)\int_0^6 \cos\left(\frac{p\pi x}{6}\right)\frac{\partial u}{\partial x}dx$$

$$\Rightarrow \frac{d\widetilde{u}_s}{dt} = -\left(\frac{p\pi}{6}\right)\left\{\left[u\cos\left(\frac{p\pi x}{6}\right)\right]_0^6 + \left(\frac{p\pi}{6}\right)\int_0^6 u\sin\left(\frac{p\pi x}{6}\right)dx\right\}$$

$$\Rightarrow \frac{d\widetilde{u}_s}{dt} = -\left(\frac{p\pi}{6}\right)\left\{[u(6,t)\cos p\pi - u(0,t)] + \left(\frac{p\pi}{6}\right)\int_0^6 u\sin\left(\frac{p\pi x}{6}\right)dx\right\}$$

$$\Rightarrow \frac{d\widetilde{u}_s}{dt} = -\left(\frac{p\pi}{6}\right)\left\{[0-0] + \left(\frac{p\pi}{6}\right)\int_0^6 u\sin\left(\frac{p\pi x}{6}\right)dx\right\}$$

$$\{Since\ u(0,t) = 0, u(6,t) = 0, t > 0\}$$

$$\Rightarrow \frac{d\widetilde{u}_s}{dt} = -\left(\frac{p\pi}{6}\right)^2 \int_0^6 u\sin\left(\frac{p\pi x}{6}\right)dx$$

$$\Rightarrow \frac{d\widetilde{u}_s}{dt} + \left(\frac{p^2\pi^2}{36}\right)\widetilde{u}_s = 0$$

The solution of above equation is given by

$$\widetilde{u}_s = Ae^{-\left(\frac{p^2\pi^2}{36}\right)t}$$

Given $u(x, 0) = \begin{cases} 1, & 0 < x < 3 \\ 0, & 3 < x < 6 \end{cases}$, so when $t = 0$,

$$\widetilde{u_s} = \int_0^6 u \sin\left(\frac{p\pi x}{6}\right) dx$$

$$\Rightarrow \widetilde{u_s} = \int_0^3 u \sin\left(\frac{p\pi x}{6}\right) dx + \int_3^6 u \sin\left(\frac{p\pi x}{6}\right) dx$$

$$\Rightarrow \widetilde{u_s} = \int_0^3 1 \cdot \sin\left(\frac{p\pi x}{6}\right) dx + \int_3^6 0 \cdot \sin\left(\frac{p\pi x}{6}\right) dx$$

$$\Rightarrow \widetilde{u_s} = \int_0^3 \sin\left(\frac{p\pi x}{6}\right) dx$$

$$\Rightarrow \widetilde{u_s} = -\frac{6}{p\pi}\left[\cos\left(\frac{p\pi x}{6}\right)\right]_0^3$$

$$\Rightarrow \widetilde{u_s} = -\frac{6}{p\pi}\left[\cos\left(\frac{p\pi}{2}\right) - 1\right]$$

$$\Rightarrow \widetilde{u_s} = \frac{6}{p\pi}\left[1 - \cos\left(\frac{p\pi}{2}\right)\right]$$

Using this result in the equation $\widetilde{u_s} = A e^{-\left(\frac{p^2\pi^2}{36}\right)t}$, we have

$$A = \frac{6}{p\pi}\left[1 - \cos\left(\frac{p\pi}{2}\right)\right]$$

Hence, we have

$$\widetilde{u}_s = \frac{6}{p\pi}\left[1 - \cos\left(\frac{p\pi}{2}\right)\right] e^{-\left(\frac{p^2\pi^2}{36}\right)t}$$

Taking inverse finite Fourier sine transform of both sides of above equation, we have

$$u(x,t) = \frac{2}{6}\sum_{p=1}^{\infty} \widetilde{u}_s \sin\left(\frac{p\pi x}{6}\right)$$

$$\Rightarrow u(x,t) = \frac{1}{3}\sum_{p=1}^{\infty} \frac{6}{p\pi}\left[1 - \cos\left(\frac{p\pi}{2}\right)\right] e^{-\left(\frac{p^2\pi^2}{36}\right)t} \sin\left(\frac{p\pi x}{6}\right)$$

$$\Rightarrow u(x,t) = \frac{2}{\pi}\sum_{p=1}^{\infty} \frac{1}{p}\left[1 - \cos\left(\frac{p\pi}{2}\right)\right] e^{-\left(\frac{p^2\pi^2}{36}\right)t} \sin\left(\frac{p\pi x}{6}\right)$$

## Exercise

1. Determine the distribution of temperature in the semi-infinite medium $x \geq 0$ when the end $x = 0$ is maintained at zero temperature and the initial distribution of temperature is $F(x)$.

   Ans: $u(x,t) = \frac{2}{\pi}\int_0^\infty \widetilde{f}_s(p) e^{-c^2 p^2 t} \sin px\, dp$,

   where $\widetilde{f}_s(p) = \int_0^\infty F(x) \sin px\, dx$

2. Use Fourier sine transform to solve the equation $\frac{\partial u}{\partial t} = 2\frac{\partial^2 u}{\partial x^2}$ under the following conditions

   (i)   $u(0,t) = 0$

   (ii)  $u(x,0) = e^{-x}$

   (iii) $u(x,t)$ is bounded.

   Ans: $u(x,t) = \frac{2}{\pi}\int_0^\infty \left(\frac{p}{p^2+1}\right) e^{-2p^2 t} \sin px \, dp$

3. The temperature u in the semi-infinite rod $0 \leq x < \infty$ is determined by the equation $\frac{\partial u}{\partial t} = k\frac{\partial^2 u}{\partial x^2}$ subject to conditions

   (i)  $u = 0$ when $t = 0$, $x \geq 0$

   (ii) $\frac{\partial u}{\partial x} = -\mu$ (a constant) when $x = 0$ and $t > 0$.

   Making use of cosine transform, show that

   $$u(x,t) = \frac{2\mu}{\pi}\int_0^\infty \frac{\cos px}{p^2}(1 - e^{-kp^2 t})dp.$$

4. If the initial temperature of an infinite bar is given by

   $$\mu(x,0) = \begin{cases} 1, & -c < x < c \\ 0, & otherwise \end{cases}$$

   then determine the temperature of an infinite bar at any point $x$ and at any time $t > 0$.

Ans: $u(x,t) = \frac{1}{\pi} \int_{-\infty}^{\infty} \left(\frac{sinpc}{p}\right) e^{-c^2 p^2 t} e^{-ipx} dp$

5. Use finite Fourier transform to solve the partial differential equation

$$\frac{\partial u}{\partial t} = \frac{\partial^2 u}{\partial x^2}, 0 < x < \pi, t > 0$$

subject to the following three conditions

I. $u(0,t) = 1, \ t > 0$

II. $u(\pi,t) = 3, \ t > 0$

III. $u(x,0) = 1$, where $0 < x < \pi$.

Ans: $u(x,t) = \left(\frac{2}{\pi}\right) \sum_{p=1}^{\infty} \left[2\left(\frac{cosp\pi}{p}\right) e^{-p^2 t} - \left(\frac{1-3cosp\pi}{p}\right)\right] sinpx$

# APPENDIX

**Beta function:** Beta function is defined by the definite integral

$\int_0^1 x^{m-1}(1-x)^{n-1} dx, m, n > 0$ and it is denoted by $B(m,n)$.

Thus $B(m,n) = \int_0^1 x^{m-1}(1-x)^{n-1} dx, m, n > 0$

**Gamma function:** Gamma function is defined by the definite integral

$\int_0^\infty e^{-x} x^{n-1} dx, n > 0$ and it is denoted by $\Gamma n$.

Thus $\Gamma n = \int_0^\infty e^{-x} x^{n-1} dx, n > 0$

**Elementary properties of Beta and Gamma functions:**

1. Beta function is symmetric i.e. $B(m,n) = B(n,m)$

2. $B(m,n) = \int_0^\infty \frac{x^{m-1}}{(1+x)^{m+n}} dx, m, n > 0$

3. $\Gamma(n+1) = n\Gamma n, n > 0$.

4. $\Gamma 1 = 1$

5. $\Gamma n = (n-1)!$, where $n \in N$, $N$ is the set of natural numbers

6. $\int_0^\infty e^{-ax} x^{n-1} dx = \frac{\Gamma n}{a^n}$

7. $B(m,n) = \dfrac{\Gamma m \Gamma n}{\Gamma(m+n)}, m, n > 0$

8. $\Gamma\left(\dfrac{1}{2}\right) = \sqrt{\pi}$

9. $\int_0^\infty e^{-x^2} dx = \dfrac{\sqrt{\pi}}{2}$

10. $\int_0^{\frac{\pi}{2}} \sin^m \theta \cos^n \theta \, d\theta = \dfrac{1}{2} B\left(\dfrac{m+1}{2}, \dfrac{n+1}{2}\right), m, n > -1$

11. $\Gamma n \Gamma(1-n) = \dfrac{\pi}{\sin n\pi}, 0 < n < 1.$

12. $\int_0^\infty e^{-ax} \cos bx \, x^{m-1} dx = \dfrac{\Gamma(m)}{(a^2+b^2)^{\frac{m}{2}}} \cos m\theta$

and $\int_0^\infty e^{-ax} \sin bx \, x^{m-1} dx = \dfrac{\Gamma(m)}{(a^2+b^2)^{\frac{m}{2}}} \sin m\theta$, where $\theta = \tan^{-1}\left(\dfrac{b}{a}\right)$.

13. $\int_0^\infty \cos bx \, x^{m-1} dx = \dfrac{\Gamma(m)}{b^m} \cos \dfrac{m\pi}{2}$ and $\int_0^\infty \sin bx \, x^{m-1} dx = \dfrac{\Gamma(m)}{b^m} \sin \dfrac{m\pi}{2}$.

14. $\int e^{ax} \sin bx \, dx = \dfrac{e^{ax}}{a^2+b^2}[a \sin bx - b \cos bx] + C$

15. $\int e^{ax} \cos bx \, dx = \dfrac{e^{ax}}{a^2+b^2}[a \cos bx + b \sin bx] + C$

# REFERENCES

1. Gupta, P. (2019) Topics in Laplace and Fourier transforms, Firewall Media, New Delhi.
   ISBN: 9789352740994

2. Debnath, L. and Bhatta, D. (2007) Integral transforms and their applications, Chapman & Hall/CRC, Boca Raton.
   ISBN: 9781420010916

3. Aggarwal, S. (2021) Integral transforms: A review, KDP.
   ISBN: 9798734162835

4. Grewal, B.S. (2012) Higher engineering mathematics, Khanna Publisher, New Delhi.
   ISBN: 9788174091955

5. Das, H.K. (2014) Higher engineering mathematics, S.Chand & Co. Ltd, New Delhi.
   ISBN: 9788121938907

6. Neil, P.O.V. (2011) Advanced engineering mathematics, Cengage Learning.
   ISBN: 9781111427412

7. Kreyszig, E. (2006) Advanced engineering mathematics, John Wiley & Sons, Hoboken, NJ. ISBN: 97804717289

CPSIA information can be obtained
at www.ICGtesting.com
Printed in the USA
LVHW060729141221
706081LV00013B/1846